MASTERS AT WORK

Becoming a Neurosurgeon

Becoming a Veterinarian

Becoming a Venture Capitalist

Becoming a Hairstylist

Becoming a Real Estate Agent

Becoming a Marine Biologist

Becoming an Ethical Hacker

Becoming a Life Coach

ALSO AVAILABLE

BECOMING A YOGA INSTRUCTOR

BECOMING A RESTAURATEUR

BECOMING A PRIVATE INVESTIGATOR

BECOMING A MIDWIFE

BECOMING A SOMMELIER

BECOMING A CURATOR

BECOMING AN ARCHITECT

BECOMING A FASHION DESIGNER

MASTERS AT WORK

BECOMING A REAL ESTATE AGENT

TOM CHIARELLA

SIMON & SCHUSTER

New York   London   Toronto   Sydney   New Delhi

Simon & Schuster
1230 Avenue of the Americas
New York, NY 10020

First Simon & Schuster hardcover edition April 2019

For information about special discounts for bulk purchases, please contact
Simon & Schuster Special Sales at 1-866-506-1949 or
business@simonandschuster.com.

The Simon & Schuster Speakers Bureau can bring authors to your live event.
For more information or to book an event, contact the Simon & Schuster
Speakers Bureau at 1-866-248-3049 or visit our website at
www.simonspeakers.com.

Manufactured in the United States of America

10 9 8 7 6 5 4 3 2 1

Library of Congress Cataloging-in-Publication Data

Names: Chiarella, Tom, author.
Title: Becoming a real estate agent / Tom Chiarella.
Description: New York : Simon & Schuster, [2019] | Series: Masters at work |
Identifiers: LCCN 2018057752 (print) | LCCN 2019000088 (ebook) |
ISBN 9781501197734 (ebook) | ISBN 9781501197727 (hardcover : alk. paper)
Subjects: LCSH: Real estate agents. |
Real estate business—Vocational guidance.
Classification: LCC HD1382 (ebook) | LCC HD1382 .C45 2019 (print) |
DDC 333.33023—dc23
LC record available at https://lccn.loc.gov/2018057752

ISBN 978-1-5011-9772-7
ISBN 978-1-5011-9773-4 (ebook)

To my brother, Pete Chiarella, a good real estate agent who worked hard in a dark time for the business. He moved on. For me, he is still a beacon.

CONTENTS

BECOMING A
REAL ESTATE
AGENT

———

INTRODUCTION

The process of buying my house began much as it does for anyone. I made a call to a real estate agent.

I was standing with my wife on a rural county road, in front of a beautiful place we wanted. The sun was setting. Tree frogs sounded in the air. I dialed the number on the yard sign. No answer. It was evening, so this didn't seem unreasonable. I called the agent who sold my last house. A young hustler who went to the local college where I'd once taught. Again, no answer. Annoying. So I decided to call the agent who'd represented the buyer of my last property. Steve Custis. I remembered sitting at the closing, thinking that he reminded me of my dad. All smiles, but dead serious about work.

That call was an act of trust. Trust in his reputation, trust in the man, trust in his profession. I was hiring someone to serve my interests. To be my representative in the matter. A real estate agent. Or, a real estate broker. Or maybe he was called a Realtor. Whatever. I had no clue about the differences. (I learned later that Steve Custis was all three.)

Over the years, I'd come to watch my various real estate agents closely, to double-check everything they did, and grew to listen to them only dimly. I tried to outthink them because I worried they weren't really working for me. I was certain they overstated their role in negotiations, and that they profited in other smallish ways that I wasn't aware of. I imagined they defined themselves that way: on sales, on moving quickly, on keeping balls in the air, while piling up commissions.

Like everyone involved in a real estate transaction, I wondered: What is a *good* real estate agent anyway? If I admit my cruelest prejudices, I'd have to own up to the fact that I saw them as a bunch of second-career, end-of-the-road desperados who'd taken a dopey course, gotten a dopey license, and then started stacking up easy cash based on sales volume.

Was it even possible, I wondered, to serve a client well without slaving to the bottom line? In fact, did any of them care about the place where they lived? Did they see their business in terms that stretched beyond the money? Aesthetic terms? Historical terms? Human terms?

What makes a good real estate agent? Who are the best

agents? Never mind that, who are the good ones? Where are they? What do they do all day? Why? Could you go into a torqued-up seller's market like the one in San Francisco or Seattle and find an agent working with honor?

I was standing outside the house we wanted to buy and I wanted answers. Here's what I found out.

The basic advertisement for the job? Real estate is a tough yet rewarding business driven by energetic, results-oriented individuals. Real estate agents must be capable of outliving the exigencies of the housing market and the pitfalls of the title process. They must use their ethical and professional training to represent the needs of their clients—whether representing buyer or seller—while navigating the sometimes-arcane processes related to the transfer of property title and deeds. Real estate agents work solely on commission. They must generate business at a level robust enough to carry them from one sales commission to the next. At times there are months between closings. Or longer.

There's freedom in it. Good agents, like the ones visited in this book, go to work on their own terms, control their own hours, dictate their own level of commitment to the job. They represent their clients but work for themselves. They do so willingly, and eagerly, and they live to see the profits.

Residential real estate agents are licensed by the state to

negotiate, arrange, and oversee the process of transferring title and deed in property sales. Their duties include listing the property for a seller, advertising that property, and showing it to interested buyers. Interpreting local and national market conditions, they strategize with clients to find the best value for the individual home buyer or seller, formulate listing offers, complete sales contracts, and oversee and interpret inspection processes and reports. They often make contacts with financial institutions for their clients and work with the title authorities to set up the closing process, then oversee that process until the property closing date, which generally takes several weeks. At closing, they get paid.

So, contacts, leads, listings, and showings. Followed by offers, negotiations, due diligence, and then the closing.

Some fail in these obligations. There's little room for sloppiness or procrastination in this line of work. The truth is, most fledgling agents don't last more than a year or two before they wash out, and even so, a bad agent can survive while not doing the job well. Their misdeeds can be difficult to track. Often only their reputation serves as fair warning to potential clients. Accordingly, some people regard real estate agents as little more than opportunistic flim-flam men. After all, anyone can sell their own home, or make an offer on a new one. A good lawyer can do the contract work and cover the transfer of deeds and title work. Many buyers and sellers resent the very presence of real estate agents and feel that the standard commission is excessive. There are apps and web service providers that tap into this sentiment, cutting real estate agents out of the equation altogether. Even so, 95 percent of American homes were bought and/or sold by licensed real estate agents in 2017. Despite popular opinion, it seems they are here to stay. So what do they do, how do they do it, and why?

Being a real estate agent has long been considered a great second career, a fine second act. It can be a good living, working on a sales commission on the title transfer of what, for most people, represents their most valued, and valuable, single asset: their home. And commissions are split in many ways: between the buying and selling agent, between the agent and their brokerage—even referring agents get a slice—so that many agents benefit from layers of income on a single transaction.

A real estate agent's success is measured in sales: frequency of sales and total sales volume, making it a different job in different parts of the country. These numbers vary wildly from one market to the next. A high-end agent in San Jose, California (where the median home price was one million dollars in 2017), might represent the buyers of a mere three properties selling at just over two million dollars each, to net themselves $200,000 in annual commissions, their end of the agent's split with the brokerage, while an agent in the rural Midwest, say Youngstown, Ohio (where the median price of homes was $75,000 that same year), might have to sell eighty properties to get anywhere near that figure. Frequency and volume. Is one a better agent than the other? Does one agent outwork the next? You'd have to hear their stories.

One of the agents profiled in this book told me, "All real estate is local." It's a different job in every part of the country, different in every decade of our recent history. Different when demand is high, different when banking conditions are favorable, different when a factory closes and demand falls away. Every agent brings their own knowledge of a given place to the job when they start. They form a sort of philosophy of the craft based on that knowledge.

For this book I chose three successful working real estate agents in three utterly different markets. Two men and a woman, each with distinct perspectives on their work in this moment in the American economy. I attempted to create a mosaic of moments that when taken as a whole, mimic the chronological cycle of most real estate transactions—from initial contacts and leads to listings, home showings, purchase offers, negotiations, inspections, and closing. This cycle is the pulse of the job, a heartbeat that runs at a different pace from one market to the next. At any time, a real estate agent, representing both buyers and sellers, might have listings in every stage of this process. In good times, it is an exciting series of procedures, negotiations, and deadlines that must be monitored, balanced, and kept on schedule. In bad times, the days between closings can stretch out interminably.

Here you will encounter a trio of representative agents. Bruce Phares is a sixty-three-year-old real estate agent and chief broker in his own partnership. He operates in Seattle, a feverish seller's market. Bruce and his partner spend weeks preparing his buyers to ready themselves for the breakneck pace of home buying, a process which ensues long before you declare yourself ready to buy a house in Seattle. It often takes less than a week before a seller has a fistful of aggressive offers, sometimes twenty or more, from prospective buyers. In representing the buyer, in a housing market where values are at an all-time high, Phares must sometimes encourage his clients to make offers that are more than 10 percent over asking price. A former jazz musician, now in his second career as a real estate agent, Phares uses his improvisational ability to wind his clients through a ruthlessly swift purchase process. A small mistake can mean tens of thousands of dollars. If he does his job well, the fiscal reward is great. But his anxiety is palpable. His sense of obligation is remarkable. He's a vulnerable, venerable soul, and sees the heart of the job as a matter of responsible representation of his client. "My client," he says, "has to be more important than the sale."

Antje Gehrken, a fifty-year-old Realtor in Chicago, has been in the business for a mere seven years. In this relatively short time she already has a thriving real estate brokerage with a dozen associated brokers spread across the city, from the northern suburbs to the Loop and throughout the South Side. She came to me recommended by the Chicago Association of Realtors, which cited her work in mentoring women Realtors who entered the field after a vital first career, or after managing a household or family. Gehrken's done all of that, leaving behind a career as the singer-songwriter for a successful regional rock 'n' roll band, which she led for more than fifteen years. She would tell you: She bounced around the stage. She cranked it up. She toured, recorded, and lived on the road. Simultaneously, Antje and her husband bought a house, managed rental properties, and raised a daughter in suburban Chicago.

Then, in her early forties, Gehrken simply stopped, left

the band, and turned wholly to a new career. First, she taught college at an art school. Then she found real estate, using the acumen developed in the management of the band, the restoration of her house, and heading up her family as her skill set. She wisely created multiple revenue streams in the residential and commercial real estate market. Now she bounces around the stage of the city, a real estate market she calls "flush, but not crazy." She provided me with a model of mentoring and self-motivation.

Finally, I turned to my local guy, Steve Custis, thirty-eight, here in my hometown of Greencastle, Indiana, population: 10,508. He heads up a local RE/MAX office in a town that has always been a buyer's market. I've been vaguely connected to Steve for more than a decade now. I even remember when he was a teenager, and in the years before that, a kid who hung out at the local skate park. "Kind of a punk," he'll tell you now. But sometime later, he left behind a job as a forklift driver in a local retail distribution plant and started to place his name on real estate yard signs for a local agency. Steve once bought a commercial investment property from a partnership I was in. That's where he set up his offices, and where he now rents an apartment to me through Airbnb. Even though he was on the other side of that sale, I was impressed by his honesty, instinct, and sense of humor. I started to see him as someone I could count on. I started asking him questions, tapping his local knowledge on all manner of issues. He pulled me into the workings of his office and his job because he knew me from around town and he expected to like my company, although I came here to Indiana from New York thirty years ago. "I'm mostly local," he acknowledged with a smile. "You, you're pretty local. And real estate is absolutely local."

These three generously allowed a writer into their processes: building leads, creating listings, assessing the markets, the buyer's showing, the seller's showing, the offer, the due diligence, the negotiation, the close. By examining the lives and minds of established, practicing real estate agents in different parts of the country, in wholly different sectors of the housing market, I discovered what makes them return year in, year out, to this difficult field, what allows them to thrive in the business, and what they draw from the job as human beings.

I tried to strip away the perceptions of the real estate agent to show the reality of the financial risks and rewards, and to determine what it takes to become what I found in each one of them: real estate agents and human beings working jobs that teach, fascinate, and fulfill.

1

CONTACTS

t's 8:41 PM on a Friday in July in rural Indiana when the phone rings. Steve Custis is sitting in front of a flat screen, sunglasses pushed back on his head. Shoes off. Cubs game on. His daughter sits at the end of the couch, still in uniform from a basketball game, scrolling through messages on her phone. On the second ring, Custis glances at the caller ID. Tom C. Tom Chiarella, that writer guy.

Custis is neither doctor nor fireman, nor pastor nor cop. Not on duty or on call. He already has a full day of work behind him, and more meetings in the morning. He knows there is nothing that cannot wait on a Friday evening, but he picks up the phone. He is a real estate agent. He learned long ago to not be annoyed. He has a set of rules about calls, texts, and emails. *All contacts are good contacts. Every contact is a potential lead.* In his business, the phone matters. Every call is the realization of a lead. Business does not go undone.

"This is Steve," he says when he answers.

There's a pause on the other end. It's a reluctance Custis recognizes. It's late. But Tom C needs something. Real estate agents like to be needed.

"Man, I'm sorry to call you so late," Tom says. Now Custis can place him. Professor at the local college. Made some money on his writing, lousy golfer, average card player. Tom. Drives a huge Chevy Silverado. Decent guy. Italian. Looks you in the eye, sometimes seemed stressed about money. What else? What else was there to remember about Tom C?

"Tom," Custis says, reassuringly. "Don't worry. It's my job. I'm always working." Names are important to Custis. He's learned that he must be able to quickly and accurately put a name with a face. He greets everyone using their names. He puts names at the beginnings of his sentences. He directs conversations by politely using names. He drops names at the end of points he's making when he wants to be heard. This is not something he's always been able to do. He never cared about people's names when he was a kid. He worked at it. He learned that from a former mentor.

"I know," Tom says, "but it's late."

"Not too late, let's hope. What's up?"

Custis knows right away that Tom has located a property. He wouldn't have called at 9:00 at night if he wanted lunch, or just wanted to flirt with getting into the market. Instinctively, Custis reaches for his laptop. He can research while he speaks. He pays sharp attention to the details, working to cipher the where, what, and why of Tom C's discovery.

Tom C launches into the story. "My wife and I were out for a drive after dinner . . ."

In the background Custis can hear birds. Or tree frogs. Tom C is outside, maybe near water. But Custis can't hear traffic. So they're out in the country. He hears someone speaking—a woman, Tom's wife. Also a professor. A singer. Drives a Nissan. *Mary*, Custis thinks. *Or Chris. Christine.*

"The windows are bad," she says softly. Custis figures they're in front of the listed house, taking their own inventory. She has gone close enough to assess the condition of the windows. *The windows*, she said. In itself, this gesture is a good measure of how much they want it.

They'll want more information. And that's easy enough. In a few minutes a real estate agent can zero in on the particulars of a property with online access to any one of several available resources, such as the Multiple Listing Service. These days, real estate is information-driven, data heavy, and fast. Custis knows these two may have accessed the basic listing information from their phones using the listing number on the yard sign.

Steve Custis doesn't care. This doesn't make him redundant. He's not worried one bit about Zillow and the instant information clients can get online. In rural Indiana, the market is still driven by a monthly printed circular that lists houses for sale in the county, agency by agency. It's an easy model, one that's worked for decades, allowing prospective buyers to browse from a magazine they pick up in gas stations, supermarkets, or diners. Custis's local RE/MAX office features about twelve pages of listings in a given month. And it costs him money to advertise that way every month too. *That's all well and good*, he thinks. But people are getting used to a world in which information on the internet is largely free.

Custis believes this information *should* be easy to get. With the basics in hand, potential clients contact him in the better half of his job, the human half, using him as a person with expertise and experience, a consultant, a potential advocate. The call from Tom is a signal of belief in Custis and his reputation. Custis likes the first uncertain moments of a call like this, when the client hasn't signed anything. And Custis is not yet attached to the potential transaction. They are just feeling him out, testing him against the facts of the listing, and his sense of the market.

For Custis, the whole encounter is an act of trust. That's why he picked up the phone. At this point there's no profit in it for him. Not yet. Though they may reveal what they want, and he may get them signed if all goes well. But tonight he will do what he does all day long: give clients his best analysis. If Tom and his wife want the house, that is if they sign with him, his best advice will follow.

"We found a house next to a covered bridge." As Tom speaks, Custis scans the computer screen, looking at the lay of the land in the northernmost part of the county. Mostly farm roads. The houses are few and far between. Big Walnut Creek snakes southward through it all.

"It's on a bluff, facing a bean field. The sun is setting over there. It's very green. There's a barn on the hill, and a deck up above the water."

Custis knows this tone of voice; Tom is lit up about this place.

"Man, Tom, you are way out there, aren't you?" Custis says, running his cursor along the course of the creek. There. He locates the bridge on the map, and the listed property is nestled against it. He can also see the price, lot size, age of home, tax rate, utility rates, and more.

"Did you look up the listing?" he asks.

"I have no data out here. My cell phone only works in this one spot," Tom says. "Which is a drawback, I guess."

"Five acres," Custis tells him. "$195,000."

He can hear Tom say, "Wow." He repeats the figure. Tom's wife hoots in the background. Custis can tell she likes that news.

"Looks like it's been on the market a little more than three months," Custis adds.

"We were just out for a drive," Tom says, apropos of nothing. "This sounds good, it looks good. But we were just out driving around."

"And you found your spot," Custis replies.

"Maybe," says Tom C, laughing.

Custis stands up, puts his wallet in his pocket.

"Maybe we should meet?" Tom says, suggesting lunch the next day, or a drink before dinner maybe.

"Nah," Custis folds up the laptop, grabbing his briefcase. It's a thirty-minute drive up there. "I'm on my way right now."

"No, Steve," Tom says. "No, no. We're good. Just wanted to get the price, find a time to see it. Tomorrow is good."

"Never as good as today though, right?" Custis says.

"Are you . . . ?" he laughs. "He's offering to come up here," Tom says to his wife.

"Oh, my god," she says.

"I just want to see what you found," Custis says. "Sounds real nice. I'll be up there in thirty-five minutes."

Tom pauses. "The sun might be down by then."

"I'll hurry," Custis says. He means it too. One thing he knows from experience is that it's difficult to show a house at night. People don't like darkness. It undoes the charm, withers the nerves.

But Steve Custis is a real estate agent. He knows the lay of the land. He jogs out to the truck. He'll make some calls on the way up there, get more information, and still beat the sun by eight minutes.

SEATTLE

It's 5:04 AM Pacific Standard Time and Bruce Phares has begun slipping into his preferred uniform: black jeans, T-shirt, collared cotton sweater, black jacket, work boots. He steps out onto his balcony, into the chilly March morning, to take a look at his Seattle.

He gives a long stare at the I-5, the great channel of freeway, which connects Seattle from bottom to top, while dividing it west to east. The highway punches straight north through the city, cutting loudly and unapologetically through downtown where Phares lives with his wife and erstwhile business partner. The I-5 flows through the myriad neighborhoods where he makes his living: Beacon Hill, South Seattle, Ravenna, Green Lake, Fremont, Greenwood, University Heights.

At dawn the highway is loud, and that matters in this business. Every week, every day, he tells someone—a newcomer, a first-time buyer, a young married couple new to Seattle home-owning—that relative proximity of a home to I-5 is a primary determinant of real estate value in Seattle. If the home is too close, you're screwed. Noise, secondary traffic, a glut of commercial property trimmed in alongside the exits—it all impacts residential value. But it's a delicate balance, because too far from the I-5 and the commute drags out, the alternate routes can get congested. Perhaps worst of all for the young Seattleite, one might feel like they're just anyone, living in any American suburb, another far flung drone, trapped by distance, rather than a Seattleite by choice.

The city throbs with growth. From his balcony, Phares takes in a skyline littered with cranes. There are six Fortune 500 companies based here and four more in the metropolitan area—including Microsoft, Starbucks, Costco, Nordstrom, Expedia, Weyerhaeuser, and the ever-expanding Amazon; and scores of corporate entities, from search engines to supercomputers to seafood. This has left the real estate market—Bruce Phares's workplace for thirty years— jammed with moneyed millennials, eager to set up steady lives in the city.

Much of Seattle's existing housing is comprised of modest bungalows built in the 20s for longshoremen, sawmill operators, and fishermen. In the years since, this housing inventory has been heavily modified and updated by generations of homebuyers who came to Seattle for any one of several emergent industries—Boeing in the 50s, Starbucks in the 90s, Amazon in the 2000s.

Land is distinctly finite in Seattle. The city sits on a peninsula. The fact that the city is nearly surrounded by water makes suburban expansion more difficult than in other American cities. New housing is gobbled up quickly.

At this moment, it is a classic seller's market. Prices skyrocket to levels unfathomable in most of the country. 1,800-square-foot Sears kit houses, the sort you might see in a nostalgic movie such as *A Christmas Story*, go on the market for $950,000 on a Tuesday, and within a week the listing Realtor will have six, eight, twelve offers, each tens of thousands of dollars above that sales price.

When real estate closings routinely take less than a week, important financial decisions are made in hours, not days or weeks. In Seattle, preparation is essential for the buyer, seller, and the agents. Phares spends weeks before actively going out on the market, training his buyers in the cultural and financial geography of the city. He often sits in long online sessions with first-time buyers transferred to Seattle as they are in the midst of starting families. They may not have even visited the city before being forced to dive into the Seattle real estate market.

AT TWENTY-ONE YEARS OLD, Phares dropped out of college and walked straight into his dream career. It was not real estate. He left school to scrap out a living playing bass violin in Seattle's lively jazz scene.

By twenty-five, he was making a living as a musician. The money was only fair, of course, but this was his calling. He could proudly say what we all want to be able to say: He was doing what he wanted to be doing. He was the kind of guy your parents warned you about.

And he loved it. It seemed like a good deal, a charmed life.

Things changed one night at a music festival in Alberta, Canada, when his hand started to hurt as he played. Cramped up. Things got worse quickly. "All of a sudden I'm telling my fingers to do stuff, and my left hand seems determined to do something else. It felt like I was losing communication with my hand."

The next night, same thing. And soon the pain was getting worse. On the third day, in the middle of a solo, his hand clamped rock hard and he couldn't hold his bass upright. Phares stayed at it, adrenaline coursing through him, fear in his throat, his life flashing before his eyes. Other musicians started looking at him in worry. Finally, he decided he couldn't finish the number. So he set his instrument down and walked off the stage.

Back in Seattle, doctors tried everything. Phares remembers the uncertainty of the time. "Everybody had their own answer: *It's this, it's that. It's a rotator cuff. It's nerves. It's blah, blah, blah.* But no doctor could truly figure it out. So, I canceled all my gigs in Seattle. I'm thirty-one, and I'm in the straights. Music is the only thing I'd done at that point. The only thing I'd ever wanted to do."

A year passed before the diagnosis came: focal dystonia, or guitarist dystonia, a rare condition often affecting musicians, in which the signals between the brain and fingers are interrupted. In 1984, there was no treatment. Phares felt that he was at his end. "I had become Bruce Phares because of my music. Without it, I wasn't anybody in my own mind. The high times were over."

He tried teaching, and stumbled between part-time jobs. He started looking at returning to college in his early thirties. Friends made suggestions of course. "At some point, my friend Loren said, 'Bruce, I could show you how to make more in a couple of months than you do in a year.' Loren was talking about real estate. About starting over doing something new, something outside my entire worldview."

Real estate seemed like the least likely answer for a guy who had never owned property. Why real estate? Now Phares doesn't hesitate. "It was the money," he says. "The lack of it. I'd trained myself to live on very little. I had lasted a long time. But then very little became next-to-nothing, and I had to make a change. I was not a salesman. I couldn't teach because I couldn't play. I was thirty-two and afraid. I needed something entirely new. A new thing, a career. And I needed it to begin quickly, not at the end of four years, or six semesters, or whatever college would have been."

Like most agents, he handled residential sales at first and made few sales in the first year. Soon his skills—finding leads, creating contacts, marketing his property listings— started to catch up to the energy he brought to the job.

Things began to improve. "In the second year, I crested $30,000 in income, and I was like, 'Whoop!' I'd never made that much money as a musician. And I remember sitting back and saying, 'Wow. I guess I had better take this seriously.'"

So the bass player with the chops became the real estate agent with his picture on a business card. Were there grumblings that he had sold out? "The musicians in my world weren't thrilled," he says, pausing. "Real estate was pretty far from the world they understood."

Even when his condition improved, calls became less frequent. Gigs dried up. His work life tilted toward daylight hours, toward understanding the needs of buyers with families, toward assessing the strengths and weaknesses of properties he wouldn't have looked twice at in his previous life. While it was painful being written off by musicians he respected, Phares wasn't used to assessing himself without music as the tool of measurement. He didn't blame the musicians.

As a fledgling real estate agent, he had to learn to measure himself in new terms. He soon discovered that the measurement was more than money. He began to think of his clients as a new commitment, a new community for him. "I couldn't be a part of the music then. I had to be a part of something new. I had to connect to other people's lives. The people I represented." He never blamed the musicians who didn't understand the shift. "People want their tribe," he says. "I've been a broker long enough to understand that now. But I still have plenty of contacts in that end of my life." Contacts? In music? Business contacts? First contacts? Leads? "Friends," Bruce says. "I should always say friends."

CHICAGO

ANTJE GEHRKEN IS A fast driver. And the sort of person who looks natural driving a Mercedes while wearing leather gloves. It's a coolness borrowed, one might believe, from her previous career as lead singer in a rock band. Only her hair—shoulder length, with a thrust of platinum blond— gives that away.

It's March in Chicago and we're headed north from the Loop, up the Dan Ryan, along interstates freshly tagged by morning rain. There's dim music on the radio, but it's hard to imagine talking music with Antje Gehrken anyway. She doesn't want to.

"I'm not a former anything," she says. "Not a former rocker, not a former singer-songwriter." Even this clarification seems irksome to her. Normally she'd be using this time to catch up on voice mails through her car's internet connection. On a regular day, she'd use her morning drive to jump from one showing to another, or to get on the phone to check in with her agents. Gehrken is a licensed real estate broker, an agent who, after further training, is qualified to employ real estate agents in a supervisory capacity.

When asked about her previous life in music, she spends a moment figuring out how little of that she wants to unwind. She's not eager to get into the past. She's over it. That's natural too.

"I'm a Realtor now," she says, passing a pack of delivery trucks headed north, up and under the slate winter skies. "That's what I am."

According to the National Association of Realtors, the typical American Realtor is a fifty-four-year-old white woman who attended some college and owns her home. 65 percent of all Realtors are women, and the majority have worked in the field for ten years or fewer. Gehrken has just turned fifty, and she's been in the business for seven years. She's an award-winning member of the Chicago Association of Realtors, who owns and operates A.R.E. Partners, a Chicago real estate office, with eight to ten associate agents working for her at any time. They buy and sell commercial and residential property in Chicago and northern Indiana and manage dozens of rental properties across the area. Before that, it was the band—recording, opening for major 80s rock bands including Heart, and touring on a bus she bought from Willie Nelson. But that stuff is in the past.

"That was a nice, nice bus," she allows, before taking a pause.

Incidentally, the word *Realtor*, which is how Gehrken refers to herself as a professional, is a trademarked, proprietary term, indicating that the agent in question is a paid member of the National Association of Realtors. While all Realtors are real estate agents (and/or brokers), all agents/brokers are not Realtors. A Realtor is similar to a real estate agent, with slightly different professional obligations and professional resources.

Gehrken admits that any first career is universally toughening; hers prepared her for the roller coaster of living through negative housing trends and the early gaps between sales commissions. "I think one of the reasons I pick myself up every day is because of my experience in the music business," she says. "You go through a lot of rejection, and then you try again. Or you have to do a show, and everything is set up, and the crowd doesn't show." She compares it to an open house, or a hot lead.

She frequently hires freshly minted, second-career Realtors, meeting them through her work in mentoring programs with Chicago Area Realtors. Many are women. It's no mystery to her why women make great real estate agents.

"What you need is enthusiasm. Organization. Local knowledge. And you have to be pretty socially adept. It helps to be a bit of a talker. That skill set is pretty much stuff women work on from the time they're eighteen. Women work harder, and longer, to be more functional adults."

She takes a call from her office, stops the car, and listens to one of her junior agents. She purses her lips, then interrupts. "We talked about this," she says. "You can't let that one go." The agent on the other end speaks for a moment. "I know," Gehrken says. "Painful. I've been there." Then Gehrken thanks her.

It might be a difficult moment in a negotiation, where the return phone call itself seems it might represent a breaking point. It might be news that a highly competitive purchase offer made by the agent on behalf of the eager clients was turned down by the seller for reasons that are unclear, or unexplained. Disappointment is a part of the process for agents, but it can be particularly hard on their clients. Delivering bad news to clients—who may be tense, eager, hopeful, desperate—is tough business. But calls cannot be put off.

"I have agents working in my firm, and sometimes they just need someone to say, 'Look, you got this. Call that person back right now.' And when they do, it's great. There's a sense of accomplishment. Because calling someone you don't know is difficult. It can be difficult to encourage a relatively new agent, one who's waiting for her first commission, when there's no regular paycheck coming, no requirement to remain in the office for long hours. When that person has been spending the afternoon calling people she doesn't know in order to develop leads, the prospect of one more phone call can really loom."

Gehrken knows that motivation must be mustered gently for agents who have yet to land their first listing, or live through their first closing. She's partly acting as mentor, and partly as head of the partnership, a person with financial gain at stake.

As broker, the office supervisor of junior agents, all she can do is give reminders and incentives to the agents to cover their bases and do their job well. They work under the umbrella of her firm, but they pay themselves through their commissions. Most people who succeed in real estate chose the field because they can control their hours and work for themselves. And as the head broker in her own firm, Gehrken, like all real estate agents, has no direct supervisor, no payroll manager, no "boss" to wag a stick at her if she doesn't do some aspect of her job.

For themselves, by themselves. Any real estate agent will tell you that the job rewards the self-starter. Young Realtors, months from their first commission, are often left to make cold calls to anonymous leads in the hope of drumming up future listings. They spend time in the cold grip of phone conversations with leads and acquaintances, setting up open houses and meet-and-greets, introducing themselves and their services to people who often didn't ask to meet them. It can be punishing for a person not used to rejection. Motivation can be an issue. Gehrken smiles. "Sometimes I just pump myself up and because I own the firm, I mean, who else do I have? Me. Just me. My employees aren't going to come in and say, 'You got this.' Sometimes I just need to look in the mirror and yell at myself and be like, '*Okay, now.*'"

She repeats, growling out the words. "*Okay, now.*"

"I dread certain calls too. We all do at the start. You're going to have to drum up business if you're a Realtor, especially when you're starting out. You have to expand your social circles. Increase your sphere of influence. You're a Realtor!'"

Gehrken knows the need to make cold calls can be a

make-or-break moment early on in the life of a Realtor. No one really wants to make them. She'll admit to that much even now. "But what choice do I have? And you can't always reveal your doubts because you're trying to lead people into battle. If they don't see that I can pick up the phone, make some decisions, get things done, then I'm not modeling anything good."

"*Okay now*," Gehrken says, thumping the steering wheel of the Mercedes. She finds a beat . . . "Return every call. Follow up every call. There's a Britney Spears song where she says it: *[You better] work, bitch!*" She sits up straighter. "I'm not above listening to that song now and then."

And a young Realtor needs to see the work, the behavior modeled. "It's important to get back to people who call about properties, even if those properties are no longer available, because then you get to ask, 'Are you represented? Are you looking for something else?'"

"What do you do with that," I ask, "if the answer is no?" Gehrken doesn't shrug, though she doesn't really know either. She is sure of one thing. "Contacts are made. You write that stuff down. Everything is just a beginning. You never know where that will lead."

2

LEADS

Bruce Phares enters a coffee shop to pick up lunch. It's a busy spot, featuring shades of humanity hunched up, shoulder-curled over their phones and laptops. Seattle, every inch of it.

Phares nods at the room. "When I was younger, there were times when I would just go to a Seattle coffeehouse to work and see if I could catch the eye of someone in the room. I'd think, *that guy looks successful.* And I'd approach and say 'You remind me of somebody I know. Do we know each other?' Just see to see if I could start a conversation."

The purpose of this foray? Phares was working to collect leads.

The accumulation of leads—names, phone numbers, email addresses—is a crucial part of the early work undertaken by new real estate agents looking to get their name out, to make themselves known to potential buyers and sellers in order to accumulate listings. After an agent is licensed, they might join a firm, but they're rarely handed their first listing and told to go out and sell it. Somehow, they have to go out into the market and find clients who are willing to let them, a novice, act as agent for the sale. For a young agent, or an inexperienced agent, this can be a mighty challenge. Creating leads is daunting, and it often involves putting oneself into uncomfortable, or at least unfamiliar, situations, such as approaching a stranger and introducing yourself. Or holding an open house for a listed property, in which every visitor is an unknown literally off the street.

"It was hard at first. I'd be sitting in an open house and I'd have thirty people walking through, and every one of them who walks in looking at me is thinking: this guy is a *real estate agent*. I would have sneered at a real estate agent once, so why wouldn't they?"

Phares hated the anxiety, the risk, the failures that grew out of these moments. But he began to see collecting leads as an important exercise. People don't sell houses often, so you can only tap your friends and relatives for business once. So the agent has to create a situation in which potential buyers and sellers get to know his name, his face, his reputation.

"What I used to do was turn it into a game, like: What

can I do to figure out the people walking through that door?" Phares says. "I'd try anything to make them pause, take a closer look at me, and think for a moment. That humanized me, I think. And funny enough, once every other open house, somebody would walk up and go, 'You seem like an okay guy. You're the real estate agent, right?' And we['d] start talking. I let them figure me out really quickly."

That makes sense at an open house, but what would be the benefit of doing the same thing at a coffeehouse or supermarket? What's the upside of gaining one contact when you're after hundreds, if not thousands?

"You get one contact and you suddenly want more," he says. "It's like you caught something, stole it from the world. Something useful that wouldn't have ever come your way if you hadn't taken a stab at catching it."

There are two ways to create leads, Phares asserts, which have to do with the stage at which you begin the career. The older person, in their second career, works into what real estate people call their existing sphere of influence. Groups where they have an existing social structure. Golf buddies. Former business associates. Fellow gym rats. The guys at your card game, your wine tasting group. These are people with whom the new agent has a reputation to trade on in order to build up their listings. These agents go after them, their friends, members of their respective sphere of influence.

If the agent is young, or new to the area, and doesn't have a sphere of influence, they have to go the other way. "Then you're basically holding open houses all the time where you meet these strangers who walk through the place, while you stand there and try to be attractive to them, in the hopes they'll pick you to be their go-to—to buy a house or list a house." He laughs at the vision of himself as a young man, standing tall in an empty house, armed only with his business cards. "That experience can make one-on-one meetings with strangers look pretty comfortable."

What do you do with the leads after you acquire them? You learn to use them. The new agent writes notes, sends emails, creates invitation lists to events using his leads. They get to know the people behind the names. They use a native curiosity to figure out how they can help clients and when the time is right.

Phares admits it's tough. "When you start out you have to learn to market your skills in any fashion, whether it's hard marketing with materials, flyers, promotional material, billboards. Or soft marketing by just showing up to everything with a smile on your face."

Phares smiles then, extra wide. "That really works," he says.

He takes his baguette and bottled water and heads to the door, looking back at the room. "In the end, you only remember the contacts you made," he says. "The rest are just friends you never had. You can't possibly miss those."

ANTJE GEHRKEN DESCRIBES THE way she saw real estate at thirty: "When I thought of real estate, I thought stereotypically. You know, an older woman with a bob haircut, and a women's business suit, maybe a little kerchief around her neck. I didn't want to be that woman, sauntering through a single family home, pointing out the sun coming in from the west or whatever," she says, flicking her hand, echoing the gesture.

Then she cringes. "But really, what kind of jerk was I to even judge?"

"This business takes all kinds," she says. "People come to this from everywhere. The truth is, I do know women like that woman now, and I really like working with them. I love them, in fact."

The world often associates real estate agents with used car salesmen and scam artists. At best, they are hustlers, out to make money. At worst, loud mouth golfers, bored housewives, and bad dentists. With poor taste in ties. People think real estate agents occupy an easy-to-get, shady second career where they proudly advertise themselves on refrigerator magnets, that they make buckets of quick money and at the end of the day aren't necessary.

Becoming a real estate agent *is* fairly easy. You take a pre-licensing course, online or in person, and then pass a state licensing exam. You then interview with a broker willing to sign a service contract in which you assign to that broker a large portion of any commissions you receive during the term of the contract (often more than 60 percent of the commission on the first sale), and in return the broker provides support in your first years in the business. So, you are splitting what you make with the person who hires you, and the remaining portion of these commissions, after taxes and overhead, will be the only money you make as an agent. Real estate agents are not allowed to work independently of a supervising broker. And there is no salary associated with this job.

However, the support of a brokerage would likely include:

- office space, desk space, office supplies, an email address, business cards, and further advertising

support and promotion (note that these costs are
usually repaid by you to the broker, through agreed-
upon fees)

- established relationships for you to utilize in the
world of insurance, title transfer, and mortgage
financing
- the assurance of qualified backup on all transactions
by a supervising real estate broker on forms,
procedures, and processes associated with the sale—
from listing to purchase offer, due diligence, and
negotiation, through the closing process.

There are no salaries or benefits associated with the
work. To restate: Real estate agents are paid only at closing.
Only when the job is done.

According to the National Association of Realtors,
51 percent of homes purchased in 2017 were first found
by buyers on the internet (whereas 30 percent were found
through a Realtor and 7 percent by yard sign). Yet I called
Custis because information is only one aspect of the need
for real estate agents. People call because they need expertise, in addition to information.

One might assume that online access to listing information
could make the role of a real estate agent less essential. Real

estate apps like Zillow, Trulia, and Realtor.com are attempting to supplant the traditional model of real estate agents working on commission by putting the entire sales process—from the initial listing through closing—into the hands of savvy home sellers, thereby eliminating the commission cost. Some have predicted these apps will spell the end of the real estate business that flourished in the last century.

Are real estate agents essential to the transfer of property? They are certainly not mandatory. Last year, often with the assistance of forward-thinking software developers like Zillow, 6 percent of all property sales in this country were classified as "For Sale By Owner." The forms used can be acquired online. The services needed (title searches, home inspections, tax queries) can be acquired that way too. The transfer of property ownership and title can be accomplished using the services of a good lawyer.

But even with the services emerging online to make buying and selling a home easier for the average customer, the fact is, at 6 percent of all sales, FSBO home sales figures were at an all-time low in 2017. Real estate agents were involved in more sales than ever. The work is there. Buyers and sellers seem to acknowledge the necessity of good real estate agents on both ends of the sales processes by counting on them so fully.

In the prevailing version of that model, real estate commissions typically run about 6 percent on the sales price of a given home. The buyer's agent receives 3 percent and the seller's agent receives 3 percent. Those portions are then typically split again, with 1.5 percent going to the listing agent (you, the individual agent in question) and 1.5 percent going to the listing broker (your firm, your supervising broker). Similarly, 1.5% goes to the home seller's agent and 1.5 percent to the seller's broker.

To illustrate:

A house sells for $250,000. You are the buyer's agent, representing a firm called, let's say, Big City Real Estate. The 6 percent commission amounts to $15,000, half of which goes to the buyer's agents and half to the seller's agents.

Home price = $250,000
6 percent commission = $15,000
Seller's net = $235,000
Seller's agent = $7,500
Buyer's agent = $7,500

$7,500 will be split by the buyer's agent and the buyer's broker, and the same is true of the seller's agent split. This split is often negotiated between the agent and his firm, so the split might run 60/40, or 70/30, but in a conventional split, the kind most often used in early transactions in an agent's career, the individual agent would receive: $3,750.

From this figure, the individual agents will pay their taxes, cover expenses, and perhaps pay a desk fee to the office as well.

Your gross income on this transaction=$3,750

Taxes=$937

Office overhead=$200

Your net proceeds=$2,613

Office fees vary, and taxes may be more or less depending on location and income. And $2,600 might be thought to be a tidy sum. But keep in mind that the average real estate agent sells four houses a year. The time between closings can drag out. And office overhead keeps piling up.

According to the National Association of Realtors, the average annual income is slightly over $41,000 per year. The Bureau of Labor Statistics places the average income for all residential real estate agents at $43,000. Now these numbers reflect the fact that many agents work part-time, and many close fewer than four houses a year. By choice.

The total income of real estate agents is driven by frequency of closings. More transactions mean more money. 80 percent of real estate agents fail in their first year. So it is fair to say, in the long-term, that the real estate agent who survives past that period is most likely the successful real estate agent in this model. His or her income is driven by his or her own effort. And with more transactions, the money starts to get good. Survival in the real estate business is often a matter of creating multiple income streams in the real estate world. An agent becomes a broker, or takes on property management, or starts an LLC to take advantage of opportunities offered by redevelopment or property improvement.

Phares, Custis, and Gehrken all make their money in a number of ways. Beyond the office, Custis has a small residential rental LLC of his own, with more than twenty properties. Phares runs a staging service, in which he fills an empty listing with furniture for the purpose of giving a buyer a sense of what the house looks like when occupied. He too has managed rentals.

Though none of them wanted to advertise their income to the world, each are thriving in their jobs, both financially and personally. It can be done.

———

So, IS THE DISTRUST deserved?

"I think it's well earned," Phares says. "I have suspicions about real estate agents too. I don't like most of them." Phares pauses, then he rolls on. "In this business, you run into people who are obviously more concerned about their commission than the client," he says. "I scroll through listings day and night, and I can always see it when some bozo takes a listing [and] puts it on the market in an unstudied way. He just demonstrates that he clearly doesn't have any understanding of what the client is after, or what he could be doing to earn the money he's supposed to be earning."

Phares is mad, but it's not about commissions. "That bozo guy makes the same commission I make, but he doesn't get the most value for his client. And that's a real thing to me." Most real estate agents, he says, value excellence in the performance of their duties with other agents.

And the lousy agents, are they just poorly trained?

"This job is mostly experience and refinement," he says. "Training is the least of it." In fact Phares discounts the learning offered in the prelicensing course entirely. "I put in, what—I don't know—thirty, sixty, ninety clock hours of just a really mind numbingly stupid class," he said. "And then I passed a fairly simple test. All that stuff that you study, and almost all the stuff on the test doesn't actually apply to the reality of real estate practice that you're going to be involved with."

"The class is not an education," he adds a moment later. "The job is."

"You do have to be a little fluid with your expectations of the career in real estate," Antje Gehrken says. "The only expectations that matter are the ones I have now. The ones I put on myself." Before the band started, she was headed nowhere near a career in real estate.

"At twenty-four, I was absolutely not interested in being a business person. And I could have never seen how real estate was anything but a business career." She wags a finger in the air. "I could never have seen that this is a relationship job first, and a business job second. In fact, it surprised me how much I liked it, right from the start."

What made it hard?

"You start out a long way from your first commission. And I'm not really scared of learning new things, but standing in front of the real estate thing, I had to say: I know nothing about this."

So she was humbled. I ask if she made lots of mistakes to start.

But she shakes that off right away. "It was different for me. I discovered I *did* know some things already. I had the experiences, I had a background. Skills. I had managed my own buildings, I had run the band, I had done all the stuff that I would have done for a client I was managing property for. I just didn't have a name, or a professional code for what I was doing. That was what the coursework offered me. Yes, I had to learn, but I had to learn to trust my experience too."

Then she looks up. "I was a rock 'n' roll girl back then," she says. "Whole different stereotype at work there. Whole different first impression."

Steve Custis too came from a kind of first career. At eighteen, he spent his time loitering and getting in brushes with the law. When he finally started working at twenty, he was doing manual labor with strict shifts that cut into his time to return to school or make a second start. So he started part-time at a real estate office after using his accrued vacation to attend the prelicensing course in Indianapolis. He scratched out the time to make showings, learned the business on his own time. "Man, when I first started out, I was working thirty-six hours at the Walmart distribution plant, operating a forklift all day, then getting out and going in to the office to check my voice mail at ten at night. I was there by myself, with no one to teach. I read every purchase agreement that went through that place. I double-checked myself against every transaction the other agents offered by day."

It was all pretty apparent to him. Custis didn't see it as a world with a lot of secrets, ones that he couldn't figure out. "I used to look at the boxes of papers and files, and I'd think, 'What is all that stuff? How can there be so much?' The boxes of old files were to the ceiling. Sometimes I'd dig in at night. And I'd see where stuff got missed, where things weren't double checked, where no one was signing off on something stupid and wasteful. I taught myself from that. I told myself I had to be my own boss there for a while, so I had to get better."

That was where Custis first considered opening his own brokerage firm.

He meets me for lunch at the local bar just off the square in Greencastle, where he's sitting in front of a pile of paperwork, which he's sneaking in before I arrive. He's nursing a Diet Coke, just tapping his pencil in the margins of one legal-sized page after another, proceeding downward toward the work—the sales price, the specifics of the contract, any peculiarities in the proposed schedule ahead—done by one of the six agents in his branch office. There's music on the jukebox, and the Golf Channel flickers on a distant television. Custis does not look hectored, or even stressed by the work in front of him.

"This is how I use my spare time," he says, as he shuffles them into a stack. He's learned to review and double-check materials in the time before meetings. It's one of his duties as the agency's broker. "When I first started, I had to check myself. Constantly. I wasn't good at it and I knew that. I didn't get much help," he says. "In my firm, I work to check them all, all the agents in the office, and I think it lets them know I'm on their side. If the sale goes through, if the customer is satisfied, if there are no major malfunctions, then it's good for both of us, for all of us." He gives me a little upnod, his signal that I should sit. "This is the middle of the sale for them," he says. "But it's sort of the beginning for me. So I take a long look."

This involves things as basic as taking a look at the sales price and comparing it to recent sales. But Custis also checks for compliance with state required inspections, inspects the written contingencies listed by his agents against the realities of a reasonable timetable. This kind of list would include the repairs and upgrades the other party has agreed to cover. He also wants to know if his agent has provided enough time for the financing contingencies required by the bank if the buyer is applying for a mortgage.

"My people get it right most of the time," he says. "But mistakes are made from time to time, sure. I'm the broker, so I have to be sure the agents aren't getting themselves in trouble here."

All the checking pays dividends for him. "A real estate agent has to know what's happening in the market all the time," he says. "This way I get an early look at appraisals on properties I've been trying to price. I get to see sales that don't go through. It all mashes up inside my head, and I get a better sense of what will and won't work."

An appraisal consists of a full inspection of the home by an independent appraiser, who uses market comparisons (similar properties sold in the last several months) and conditions to determine the cash value of the home at closing. Most banks require that the appraisal meet, or exceed, the sales price. This is a check against overpricing, price inflation, and fraud.

The purchase contract, like the ones Custis is checking, is the most perilous point for a new agent. A second pair of eyes—in the form of a more experienced agent—passing over every offer sheet is generally welcomed by agents working under a broker like Custis. It's a function of the broker. It is a part of his licensing, and an aspect of his responsibility. It is no skin off his teeth as team leader. "Now, I can read an offer sheet pretty damned quick. It's second nature. If I don't look things over, well that's just lazy. So, I look before I call, before I meet with my client, or I remind my agents to. I like to be easy with the facts about a sale. Not lazy. Easy. Easy to access, easy to call up."

It's a lesson he learned in his first real estate job. "At my previous firm, it was sink or swim. Kind of like they wanted you, the agent, to make less work for them, one way or another. Like, do it right, or you will be gone. There was no learning."

Our lunch arrives. "And yeah, it's work, not school. But a real estate agent has things to learn every day. Every drive to work, past every house, is learning. Real estate agents have to watch the world they live in."

3

THE OFFICE

Real estate agents deal in the negotiation of space. Who owns it, who repairs it, who lives in it, who answers for it. So it's ironic that Bruce Phares doesn't care much about the space he occupies in his own business. He heads up a small partnership (the remnant partnership he started with his wife, Donna Bertolino, more than a decade before) that now includes another agent named Mark Besta. This partnership works under the umbrella of a large regional agency called Windemere Real Estate. There are at least nine Windemere offices in Seattle. Windemere provides advertising, office space, and administrative support to a partnership like Phares's in exchange for a commission cut, rent, or an office service fee.

The average real estate agent in this country has been in the business for ten years, but with their current firm for only four years. It's not uncommon for real estate agents to move around over the course of a career, to step out on their own, or to team up with agents they know or admire. Most work for larger agencies on two-year contracts, and as they gain experience, it's natural that they would want more control over their time and prospects. Phares's partnership with his wife was a stand-alone operation for ten years. He calls it "a computer with a view."

Phares rarely, if ever, brings clients to the office. Files pile up there. Books. Sheafs of floorplans sit untended on the credenza. Old volumes of the journal *Real Estate Law* stack in a corner. He pshaws in their direction. "It's hard to learn anything about this business from a book," Phares says. "I mean, no, that's not right. I myself didn't learn from books. I learned from experience. I never even cracked those things. All these years, I never opened them. Never had to."

It seems hard to believe that he would never have to consult *Real Estate Law* after thirty years in the business. "When I need to consult someone," he said, "I call a lawyer. Or I talk to a senior colleague. Besides, that whole journal is available online anyway. So I always have it with me." He taps the phone in his pocket, which alerts him, so he takes it out to check his emails.

"I want them out in the city when they're here." He wants them looking at the physical truths of Seattle. He doesn't want them looking at him. He doesn't FaceTime or videoconference either. He speaks, tells the client what he's learned. Phares is content to be the narrator; the buyer is the protagonist.

To better serve clients, Phares and Besta try to limit themselves to five active buyers at a time, and they maintain a pipeline that brings their buyers into the market in a controlled progression. Besta works from the office as a liaison with the banks and schedules the home inspections and the closing. Phares works the locations and does the meetings and showings.

New buyers often fly in from Dallas or Salt Lake City with young children in tow for three days on a visit paid for by their new employer. They start at a listing site with their feet on the ground. They have questions. Phares tries to answer them on the spot. But he'll call Besta to get an answer on the timing of an inspection when he needs it. Real estate agents need to be able to jabber freely and authoritatively about factors such as ease of access to water, the variety of views, the presence of recreation centers and parks, access to the airport, and school districts.

The roiling demand for housing in Seattle leaves Phares unable to keep a calendar more than a day or two out. When a new house drops on the market, he usually discovers it in the early morning, and if he believes it might be right for a current client, he'll often have made his preliminary walk-through by noon. This may involve livestreaming or recording video for a client who can't join on such short notice.

He asks if I want to sit where there is more elbow room. "We can go upstairs," he says. "I sometimes do meetings in the conference room upstairs," he explains, while replying to another email. "But I want to be out in the city with the clients, not crouched in the office."

STEVE CUSTIS'S OFFICE SITS on the main floor of a converted nineteenth-century mercantile building on the southwest corner of the town square in Greencastle, a town of about ten thousand. There's a beaver in the storefront window. And a beehive, and a stuffed fox. The beaver is stuffed and turned to face inward, toward the office, so that it appears to be looking over his shoulder when Custis talks to you. Custis trapped it on a property several miles south of town.

His desk is spartan. Two squares of Post-it notes. Family photos. A pair of empty folders. No lamp. No art on the wall. A splay of pens. A pair of computers. No extra paper.

Custis has been in the space for a year and a half, but it looks in some way temporary, like an office freshly rented, a hotel business center where guests occupy the space for an afternoon. It doesn't look anything like home. Real estate brokers may be in the business of buying and selling places but they don't seem to occupy space themselves. Their work is entirely portable. They take it with them, in cars, under arms, in satchels.

Custis bought a property from me once. I was the seller, represented by an agent I'd used before, the young guy everybody in town swore by. Custis was the other young gun in town. An up-and-coming real estate broker, committed to opening a RE/MAX franchise in this little Indiana town. I liked the way he worked and the stories he told. He never made excuses. Never prevaricated. He just moved forward toward the sale again and again. He was a real pain-in-the-ass on an outdated alarm system. My partners and I knocked our price down because of it. Slightly. It seemed fair.

He never lied and he never did one thing when he claimed to be doing another, not that I could see. In the end, I was happy to walk away from the deal my partners and I made with Custis, though we barely broke even. Real estate in rural Indiana is hard. Supply is small, scaled down to the population. And the demand? Smaller still.

"Someone always wins a real estate deal," Custis told me in his office later on. "The trick for an agent is to be sure you create a win for your client. I wasn't working for you then. I couldn't possibly do that for you."

He sits behind his desk and looks at me levelly. "When you watch a real estate agent work," he says, "it may not seem like much is happening. Nothing happens in the office really. It'll just be me, on the phone."

What would he be doing? What sorts of tasks?

"One thing I like about this job, every phone call is completely different. Every time. Mostly I work to settle things down."

To "settle" things?

"People get rattled when they buy or sell their house. I just have to reach out from the office, and settle things. You'll see, I guess." He looks around his office, as if there might be a television to distract me. "There's not much to look at," he says, looking over his shoulder, at the beaver. And the beehive. "But these calls matter. The office holds things together I guess."

Moments later, he has something to show me. "Look right here," he says, with a wry grin, sliding a newsletter-type thing from RE/MAX's corporate office across the desk. "Top two hundred RE/MAX agents in the country

for February," he says. He puts his finger on the picture of a young guy I don't know, and a woman I recognize from her signs around town. "Two of our agents listed right there." He claps his hands, rubs them together.

Custis worked for several years as an agent for a local brokerage, then opened the RE/MAX office in Greencastle. Unlike Phares, who runs a partnership in a side regional sales office, or Gehrken, who started her own office in Chicago, independent of a national chain, Custis elected to join the large national real estate sale franchise. And RE/MAX is the biggest, controlling the largest share of the residential real estate market in the United States and Canada since the 1990s. Founded in Colorado in 1973, by two entrepreneurial agents, RE/MAX is now the world's largest real estate company, with 120,000 agents in seventy countries worldwide.

Custis likes the brand recognition of RE/MAX, the network of contacts provided by the corporation, and its online tools. The national franchise structure also allows Custis to access corporate resources, including training seminars and training materials for a single fixed-cost investment on his part, which depends on the size of potential market size.

RE/MAX franchises price out between $40,000 and $280,000, depending on the market potential of the area.

The amount covers inventory and supplies, office furnishings, setup and signage, with ongoing costs per agent—desk fees, renewal fees, annual fees, much of which Custis chooses not to pass onto his agents. Additionally, 1 percent of the gross monthly sales by the office agents goes back to the corporate office. When it comes to a franchise with national recognition, the costs are not minimal. But it comes with the right to use the RE/MAX logo and corporate resources—associated 800 numbers, websites, networks of contacts, and lists of leads based on internet traffic.

"See, now I'm going to make something out of this," he says, of his agents being listed in the RE/MAX top sellers national newsletter. And in the next ten minutes, he gets to it, updating the company's Facebook page with the info, handwriting each of them a quick congratulations, then calling to make a date to take them both to lunch. He narrows his eyes and thinks it through. "I'll do something more too," he says. "Each of them will get a bottle of something. It's not enough, but you have to notice. Real estate agents notice everything, on both ends. That's the job."

4

LOCATION

Sitting in his glass-walled office, in the Capitol Hill neighborhood of Seattle, Bruce Phares works from two computer screens—a satellite image on the right, and a database of pin-pointed real estate transactions on the left. He comes at Seattle from above, then moves north to south . . .

"To understand the city," he says, jerking his cursor to and fro, cup of coffee in his other hand, "you need to know that the city was built by receding glaciers, and we consequently have all these different hilltops left behind. And the lake was carved out by it, Puget Sound was carved by it, and when the water came back in, this is what we were left with."

The good agents are historians of place. They know where the pool halls were. Where the mudslides happened. They understand the lives a house has lived since its construction, the development and growth of neighborhoods and cities. They also understand the intricacies of local gov-

ernance and zoning. They know rudimentary construction techniques. These are the details of location.

Bruce Phares starts the same way with each new client: looking down on Seattle from the perspective of a satellite. He throws that view up on a shared computer feed and slowly moves in on the geography while talking to his new clients on the phone. Speakerphone, usually, because generally these meetings are virtual, set up with a client who has yet to move to Seattle, or one who is only just preparing for a dip into the market.

Phares can sound more like a liberal arts professor than real estate broker. He has a deep and arcane sort of knowledge of Seattle, which apparently includes some expertise in the Northwest's glacial era. But as we know, there is no college degree required to sell real estate in this country. Nationally, 30 percent of Realtors possess a four-year college degree. In fact, there are still states where you don't even need a high school diploma to get a real estate license. And Bruce Phares is less geology professor than he is a knockabout guy. He grew up in Seattle. He dropped out of college after a semester and worked as a jazz musician.

So why does he start his client preparation with the geology of the place? How will that save them money? Or make him money?

"Because in places along the shoreline of this city, the shore is very steep and unlivable," he says. "Houses were built there before construction standards were up to the task. Beautiful views, but they must be avoided. And the shore is too sandy and friable in other spots. Not good for construction, even now."

Phares zooms in on sites where the soil composition has created problems in home construction. The houses that still stand, he says, are an endless labor of love. They should have never been built.

He tilts the surface view of the earth, and cursors in on the fist-shaped piece of land known as North Seattle. "So you have the north side of Seattle, basically everything above this waterway, which they call 'the cut.'"

"You have to know what forces created the place you live in," he says. "So you can know what your house was built on. This stuff is pragmatic, not exotic. I don't want a client buying where the constitution of the land won't support the foundation of a building." He takes a mouthful of coffee and swallows. "So, glaciers. Yeah."

Consider the real estate agents classified as "farmers." These are agents who exclusively work in one neighborhood, one town. They become fixtures by working more traditional marketing techniques such as postal mailings,

billboards, promotional magnets and printed circulars left in local restaurants. An agent like this might farm a single subdivision for a generation using this model, which is considered old-fashioned by today's standards. And while all real estate agents are prohibited from speaking about their competitors in any evaluative way by the standards of their state licensing boards, Phares clearly admires these farmers. He avails himself of their knowledge of local markets as best he can, in partnership with them. These are the most local members of his profession. Foot soldiers.

"They know everything. They've been doing it for years and years. Their signs are up all over the neighborhood. They know the drainage patterns. They have all this geology internalized. The scheduled roadwork. The way the sun falls into every living room. They're not going to go off that turf. They are the masters of their location, of *that* location."

Phares does not count himself among their numbers. He and agents like him refer to themselves as "free agents." He goes into the world looking for discoveries that match the needs of his clients. "I work wherever my client wants to go, as long as it's in the bounds of where I can ethically be of service." The entire map of Seattle is a kind of territory to him then. "If someone wanted to go to Lynnwood"—he

clicks on a point sixteen miles north of Seattle—"I couldn't help them much. A real estate agent who says he can work anywhere at all is taxing credulity. I'd be hard-pressed to be good counsel as to what agents are seeing up there," he says, while clicking in to look at a pair of listings in Lynnwood. "But I do know who the farmers are up there. I would know who to ask." Knowing people, creating contacts, staying in touch—these are the watchwords of a real estate agent. It works best locally.

Because real estate is local by nature, it demands knowledge and valuation of place in local terms, on a local scale. That's why individuals turn to real estate as a second career, much of the time in markets where they grew up.

"An agent has to understand the standards and practices of a specific place or set of places, the ebbs and flows of a specific *street* in certain cases. I *am* local to this city. A farmer is local on a different scale. Expertise applies only within our limits. Physically, I mean. In that way, we're all farmers. Place is part of who we are."

Phares drops in overlays on the map, and properties start to pop up on the screen. Using filters, he color-codes to reveal fluctuations of property value between neighborhoods, then drops a dartboard pattern of recent zoning variances, a grid map of recent street work, the glowing electrical grid.

Phares is fluid with the movement between the layers of information. In seconds he can show the impact of over-lapping school districts on three-bedroom starter homes, or highlight the limitations of commercial development adjacent to neighborhoods designated L-1 (low-rise residential). It's tempting to believe we are seeing his true medium. But Phares is quick to correct.

"There's a whole field in the development world, where this is what they do," he says. "They've got maps on their wall, everything's color-coded. Everything is a pattern or trend." Phares thinks of himself as more of a brick-and-mortar guy. He likes to lay his eyes on a property. "That's just not me. I do this presentation to warn our clients: there's a lot to absorb in this city, and you have to move fast."

He looks up, through the interior window that encloses his office, and thinks for a moment about the essential nature of his job. "I remind myself sometimes that I'm trying to help people find the place they want to put their feet down in at night, a single spot in one of these swaths of color. But I want them to see the big picture of Seattle, so they'll understand why we have to be 10 percent over the asking price in this market. Minimum."

The old cliché about real estate—*location, location, location*—matters in a different way to Phares. He believes

in understanding a place by standing in it. "You can't buy a house based on photographs from a listing sheet, or everybody would be doing it," Phares says. "I make people stay in the backyard of a house they want. They have to listen. People forget, real estate is a sensory thing. If it's too loud, we wait, no matter how much they love the kitchen or whatever. And that becomes a lesson we learned. It makes them a better, more informed buyer for next time. Location is everything."

Glaciers are local. Geology pragmatic. So it makes sense that real estate agents are most powerful on a local, pragmatic scale.

5

SHOWINGS

RESIDENTIAL

PHARES IS DOING A showing for out-of-town clients: a couple moving back to Seattle from Marin County, California, after an initial retirement a year ago. They're in town for a day, and want to take a look at a smallish three-bedroom in Wedgewood, a desirable northeastern section of the city. They're going back to work. The woman will start back at Microsoft; her husband will work from home as a software security consultant.

Since Bruce has partnered with them before, we arrive before they do, and Bruce gains access to the house via a coded lockbox hung over the door-handle. Real estate agents use these lockboxes to stash the appropriate keys, providing access to other agents, who get the combination by calling to announce their intention to visit. The listing agent leaves

an entry log at the house (more contacts, more leads) for the buyer's agent to sign. This frees up time for both parties, and allows for more traffic by potential buyers. Phares slips off his shoes at the door, because he knows the clients do the same in their own home. He circles through the house to see how it matches up to the listing sheet. Pretty nicely, it turns out. "It's a good description," he says of the listing. "It doesn't overstate coziness as a way to make up for the lack of space." He finds and picks up a grocery bag in an otherwise-empty bedroom, then returns to survey the living room.

He knows instinctively that this house will not suit them. But they are on their way, and every showing can teach you something about a client. He's going through with it. They asked to see the house. "This room," he says, "will undo it. The husband is a serious audiophile. I mean, *serious*." The front room doesn't offer enough space for even the first speaker setup. And the kitchen is small. "They like to cook for each other," he says. Phares knows it's important to know a client's habits and preferences. He watches the way people live to see how a house will fit them.

Phares is not always negative. He just knows how to boil things down. There's no disappointment in his voice. It is his job to catalogue details and he is unbearably quick, trusting

gut. Disqualfiers matter too. His clients asked for this wing, so they must have seen something in the adversement, or they knew the neighborhood well enough to be drawn to it. He doesn't mind working to understand their motivation for driving forty miles to look at a 1,900-square foot house with no notable landscaping, ugly siding, and a cement driveway buckling from beneath.

Phares applies his sight test to the smallest particulars of a space.

He's never seen this property before and the listing report was only vaguely helpful. He reads the place quickly. He sees what is and isn't working. In his initial seven minutes there, he notes the following, out loud:

- No windows on the north side of the house.
- Only a one-car garage.
- Backyard: mushy and wet.
- The foundation is too short to adequately support expansion to a second floor.
- There's no room in between the front door and those cement steps to the driveway, so no room to expand the first floor either.
- Lousy appliances.

Does the showing feel like a waste of time? "There no such thing as a waste of time with a good buyer. I've been with these two on a dozen showings," he says. "I learn something every time we do one. They were attracted to this place. So, it's my job to understand what made them want it, and to use that information."

Bruce greets the couple warmly when they arrive. The woman gives him a hug. She's a scarved, elegant figure. Jane. The man holds out a hand. He's an older white guy, with a neat haircut, wearing chinos. He renamed himself after a Sufi mystic poet ten years ago. Yunus.

Immediately, the three of them—two buyers and their agent—begin walking the house, dodging one another in the hallways, turning corners at an unexpectedly fast pace. Jane takes an extra-long look at the heavily shaded backyard. "Wet," she says to herself. Throughout the process Phares stands back to give them room to move, but stands within earshot, occasionally calling out facts about the structure and its detailing. "The roof is about halfway through its life. ten to twelve years left," he says. "The boiler is new, 2015 anyway."

Yunus calls out questions as the two men drift forward toward the living room. Jane looks out the window. "The best house Bruce ever sold us was the one we lived in at the

time," she tells me. I assume she's talking about a rental, but there's more to it than that. "He first sold me that house in South Seattle in 1996; then Yunus and I got together not long afterward, and we wanted something bigger." She turns to me, shakes her head a little. "God, Bruce must have taken us to look at one hundred houses that summer . . ."

Yunus, who's heard the tail end of her story, calls out the next sentence as he re-enters with Bruce, in what must be a familiar sequence. "And then, finally we got it!"

Jane smiles. "Yes. And then finally, I said, 'Okay, we got it!' We found a new place we wanted to buy. I declared: 'This is a great house.' And Bruce just said . . ."

"That's a terrible house," Bruce finishes the thought from doorway to the center hall.

"Right! A terrible house!" she says, looking at Bruce, earnestly. "Yes, that's what he said."

What made it so bad? What was the disqualifier?

"It was seriously overpriced for the neighborhood," Bruce says.

"They had done a bunch of crazy things on the remodel," Jane adds. "There was charm to it, but we were going to have a miserable time living in it."

"It had a bathroom the size of a postage stamp!" Yunus chimes in.

Jane picks up the thread then. "So we argued a little, and finally Bruce digs out his phone, punches in a phone number, and hands it to me. He says: 'Talk to Bill.'"

Bill who? Was this a setup? Was Bill an agent representing another listing?

"Bill the builder! Bill, the guy Bruce trusts!" says Jane. "We talked for an hour about renovating the house we were *already* in. We talked about staying put."

"And then we hired him," Yunus adds.

Jane smiles then. "So Bruce sold us on our own house. And he walked away from these huge commissions," she says. "He lost two sales that night. The new place and the one we would have sold later. And we just remodeled our current house."

"And it was then one of the most beautiful houses in that entire region," Bruce says.

"A total silk purse house," Jane says, "I don't know how that happened, exactly, but we credit Bruce. And years later, he sold it for us again."

"That was in a down market," Bruce says.

"Sixty thousand dollars over asking," Jane says, "with buyers, you know . . ."

"Competing," Bruce says.

"Right," she says. "Competing buyers."

"We got an offer the first day from a couple who didn't even want to look at it initially, because it didn't have enough bedrooms," Jane says. "They ended up buying it. Amazon people. That was five years ago, and that house is now worth a million and a half. We couldn't ever buy it back, but anyway. I'm telling a long story because our real estate agent did that. Our Bruce."

Phares is smiling. He likes the story and seems genuinely fond of the couple. "You accrue a lot of moments in a real estate career where the best result for your client is not the best financial result for you," he says later. "You move forward. You do what's right for them. And it's not that hard, because the job of a real estate agent is to protect their interests, to represent them. I am *their* agent." The return for this sort of ethical conduct? "They tell that story," he says, "and I'm happy for them every time. And they have given me repeat business a couple of times over in the years that followed."

Back in the living room, shoes off and the story told, they look at each other once more, and Jane says, "well, this house doesn't work at all for us."

"Right," Bruce says.

"Right," Yunis calls back, nudging his toe into a shoe. And they are done with this one place.

COMMERCIAL/MIXED USE

THE CHICAGO SKY IS a flaming winter blue. Antje Gehrken's Mercedes sits in a decaying parking lot in the northside suburb of Waukegan. Gehrken stands at the rear of her car, changing shoes. Slips off her dress shoes, replaces them with a pair of ankle-high zip-up 80s boots caked in mud. Dress shoes once, now trashed, you might say. There's a plunger in the trunk too, its head buried in a plastic shopping bag. She grabs it and shuts the trunk.

This is a commercial real estate showing. She represents the seller, a bank forced to foreclose six months prior. She is working alone today, as agent to the seller. Gehrken's firm, A.R.E. Partners, primarily lists residential sales, with occasional crossovers into small commercial offerings.

As a real estate broker, Gehrken has the designation which allows her to operate in commercial real estate. So a day like this one, showing the former childcare center (and mixed-use building), is not beyond her ken. But she prefers the chemistry of residential real estate.

Commercial real estate is classified as property that brings or has the potential to bring income. It is non-residential, which means that it's not being purchased as a residence for the buyer. In most states, a commercial real estate agent requires additional training. The field is more lucrative, however. The average residential Realtor made a little more than $41,000 in 2015 (a figure that includes all real estate agents, including those who only do the job part-time), whereas the average commercial real estate agent netted $135,000 in the same year. The reasons are myriad. Title work is more complicated, financing plans are more speculative. Zoning requirements (parking specifications, fire suppression, signage, shared maintenance, and more) can be a tangle. Commercial real estate properties are most often far larger than traditional residential ones (think square feet). And the price of commercial real estate is generally far higher than residential property because of income potential.

While 63 percent of residential Realtors are women, industry estimates show that women make up only 35 percent of the commercial real estate agents, with the majority of them working in asset management rather than active sales. Commercial real estate agents make more money, and in commercial real estate, men average $150,000 a year, whereas women average closer to $130,000. The gender gap is undeniable.

Gehrken doesn't want to fight that battle. She sees it as a reinforcement of why women gravitate to residential sales. "Women work for themselves in residential real estate. What they make is clearly tied to the effort they give it, without anyone getting in the way," she says. "In this job, I move around, and work my own hours. I talk to a lot of people all day. That's what I want from the work." Commercial real estate feels male to her. "It's pretty corporate. Pretty hormonal. It feels more like an office sport."

Beyond that, the jargon of commercial real estate is unfamiliar to most homebuyers. It's loaded with terms such as "triple net lease" (in which the renter agrees to pay the owner's retail insurance, real estate taxes, and the shared maintenance on a commercial space). And the value of commercial real estate is expressed in dollars per square foot, since the bottom line of commercial real estate is tied to the presumption of rent as the primary income.

For instance:

A 3,000-square-foot retail auto parts store renting for $8,000 a month would be said to rent for $32 per square foot.

$96,000 ($8,000 X 12 months)/3,000 square feet= $32 per square foot

And $32 per square foot might be a bit high in Buffalo, New York, where the average price of retail commercial rent is currently $26 per square foot, but it would be an insanely low price on Miami's legendary retail corridor, Lincoln Road, where retail rents average $250 per square foot, or upper Fifth Avenue in Manhattan, where the average is $3,900 per square foot.

Real estate markets are local in their first measure.

In real estate development, properties are sold with the idea of reinventing their use. It takes a vision that looks beyond what was left behind. "My client is the bank," Gehrken says. "but I'd like to see whoever ends up in this space succeed." She takes a long look through the front window, toward the street. "Vacant commercial space kills a neighborhood like this. There's no foot traffic, no coming and going, no familiar faces, and fewer tax dollars. It makes life harder for everyone."

Just as in residential real estate, commercial foreclosure comes when the mortgagee can no longer afford to keep up payments on the mortgage. Gehrken is involved here as receiver, a court appointed individual with the custodial responsibility for the property. On her last showing, Gehrken raked the front lawn beforehand. "I found six bucks too," she told me, "just sitting in the grass." Receivers displace the property owner as the active property manager and make all decisions regarding management and operations. They collect whatever rent is due from tenants, find new tenants, and maintain the physical space for a fee. Gehrken's partnership is also the listing agent for the bank sale of the building.

Potential buyers look into commercial spaces with a business plan in mind, if not in hand. Each one has different needs than the last. Gehrken's job is to translate the facts of the physical plan (the dimensions, the room layout, the occupancy rate, the income pattern and potential) and the history of occupancy ("This building was built in 1976; it housed a barbershop for twenty years, then a hardware store . . .") with an open mind as to what it might become. She wants to get as aggressive a price from the buyer as possible, without leading them into anything.

"I've learned to be less enthusiastic about the idea than the person who has it," she says. "I just try to give them the facts."

The facts one should know about the property today include:

- This building is a former childcare center.
- 11,000+ square feet on a corner-lot streetfront.
- Two rooftop apartments rented to long-term clients, and another one vacant.
- On the first floor: three former retail spaces, connected by ill-considered doorways, pass-throughs.
- One space is filled with leftover cribs.
- There's a garage, with boxes of picked-over tools, a pile of old tires, and political signs left over from an election six years ago.

- There's an office off the side of the garage.
- The two existing apartment leases pull in $1,300 a month, which becomes more like $2,000 a month when the third one is in service.
- The building is heated on a boiler system. The boiler is fifteen years old, which is considered midlife.
- Out back, there's a ten-yard Dumpster, which the neighbors have filled with trash.
- There's a smallish, deserted playground surrounded by plank fencing, and a ten-space private parking area.
- And an old diaper in the alley.

Several weeks ago, Gehrken hired a group of single mothers from the neighborhood to clean up, letting them take what they wanted for their own children after the job was done. It's the kind of measure of the local good a receiver can do for a property, since decision-making lies in her hands.

Although Gehrken nets a monthly fee as receiver, she knows that it would be better for everyone if the building sold today. Better for the bank, since the proceeds would be applied to the remaining debt on the property. Better for the surrounding neighborhood, since an unoccupied building hurts property values. Better for the building itself, since an occupied space is a vital space that gets the daily attention of its occupants. And better for her firm, given the possibility of the sales commission.

As Gehrken walks swiftly through the first floor of the building, she outlines the financial situation today, in a brief rehearsal of the showing.

The asking price is $350,000. There's one existing offer, under $300,000, a little too low for the bank's liking.

Real estate agents need a lithe mind and strong short-term memory. Gehrken spins these facts without looking at any listing sheet, without checking her computer, without the help of bullet points. She moves to straightening up one room, then another, while framing the prospects of the property she represents with a comprehensive, gut-level understanding of the business of the property and the business that closed. She knows this stuff as landlord, as developer, as a broker and agent. From memory.

She got here fifteen minutes early because the maintenance guy told her the sink in the basement wasn't draining. The basement floor was partially flooded too, he said, because one of the feed lines to the boiler was dripping. She puts on her mud boots. Gehrken wants to take a shot at breaking through the clog with the plunger.

"Getting that sink to drain would be great," she says, on our way down the wide wooden basement stairway. "That's just one more little job that would be done. One more thing a buyer won't be adding up against the price."

A deserted daycare. You could tear it down tomorrow, and no one would miss it. But in the right location, this same structure, at this same price, would be a steal. In the right location this would make a fabulous restaurant or craft brewery.

The trick with real estate, Gehrken says, is to never see past location. The location *is* the value. "The street tells the story," Gehrken says. "Look. It's a sunny day in winter, and no one is out walking. That's the story of this place." She shrugs.

She knows you can't reinvent a place based on what you wish it were.

"In real estate, you very rarely don't know exactly what you have," she says. "The sale of this property is mostly a matter of finding a buyer who wants the income from the apartments, and has a new idea for the commercial space. It should be someone local, who knows the neighborhood, the location." She stares at the empty street. "Or something about the location, so many people, so much traffic, so many houses turning over on the market, that the place invites speculation on what it might become." Obviously that isn't the case here. This building has been on the market for several months.

Down in the basement, next to a boiler, the sink is still dripping. Gehrken pulls off her leather jacket, leans into the plunger and works the blockage. Nothing. She tries again. "I am stubborn," she says, but nothing happens. She tries again. The water isn't going anywhere.

Minutes later, the buyer arrives for the showing.

Gehrken meets him at the door. He's a Hispanic guy in his mid-forties, head of security for a local school district. He's wearing a golf shirt with a school logo stitched to it. He's on his lunch break, so he's got an hour. He's by himself, no agent at his side. Gehrken is low key; she hands him a copy of the listing sheet that includes significant figures— the tax bill, cost of utilities, monthly rent, water bill, the makeup of the HVAC system, type of roof construction, number of bathrooms, kitchens.

She explains that she represents the bank in this case, that they have an offer in hand and that they are reserving him time to make one himself should he see fit. She explains the schedule: he has two days to decide. But she urges him to move at his own pace. And then they walk.

They climb to the roof. Gehrken tells him both tenants pay their rent on time in the apartments up there, that she's never seen the inside of either and the third apartment would raise monthly income to $2,000. She's aware that the rental income would provide a major screen against a commercial mortgage. Income screens are used by owners in mixed-use spaces as a means of leveraging mortgage costs or construction loans. Extra money from rent might pay for the commercial mortgage that might be used to finance the purchase. If the commercial mortgage were to run at $3,300 a month, the rental income would reduce that cost to $1,300 a month.

"I have cash. I won't need financing," the potential buyer says. A cash buyer. So, no mortgage. No waiting period for financing. The kind of thing a real estate agent likes to hear, because setting up a mortgage can add weeks to the closing process.

Gehrken nods, seeming nonplussed by the news. She doesn't ask what he's considering using the space for, not right away. She is waiting, listening. Real estate agents are not allowed to "puff" the aspects of a property that might particularly appeal to a buyer. This ethical constraint runs contrary to the movie stereotype of real estate agents as flashy, garish salesmen.

For instance, Gehrken can't say, "This room would make a great dining room for your restaurant." But she can detail the plumbing capability and electrical layout, or confirm that zoning patterns don't prohibit a restaurant there.

"What are the measurements in this room?" the man asks.

Gehrken checks her floor plan this time. It's close to nine hundred square feet, she says, including the pass-through to a kitchenette.

"I'd like to have a community space," the buyer explains. "Something people in the neighborhood can rent for weddings and parties."

Gehrken likes this idea, and points out that the garage and loading dock adjoin the space from the rear, making deliveries particularly easy. Her familiarity with the place is a strength. It feels as if she were thinking with the perspective of someone who had worked the space for years.

The buyer's wife is a tax preparer, who runs an office that expands rapidly during tax season. He wants the other two retail spaces for her business.

Gehrken outlines which of the dividing walls in those spaces might be load-bearing, and so might be removed to create a single larger space. "But you'll want to check that for yourself," she says. She can get him in touch with a contractor to double-check things.

He's there for nearly the whole hour, and says he'll want his wife to take a look before he decides.

After he leaves, Gehrken confesses, "I liked that man. He's got ideas for making the space useful to that community. It's irresistible. But he's got to be his own counsel. I can't represent him. He should get an agent just to consult with."

It's clear why she must remain circumspect. She's operating in a distinct buyer's market. She represents the seller.

"You can't work for anyone but your own client," she says, grabbing her coat and the plunger in the plastic bag. "There are a lot of empty spaces like this in the neighborhood. I have to remember that. I have to remain a little distant. You can't be half-assed with your obligations to your client. I represent the bank."

That said, she admits she's rooting for him.

A VIRTUAL SHOWING

IT'S A SMALLISH, TWO-STORY Tudor in East Montlake, a Seattle suburb. Asking price: $880,000. Oldish roof, limestone exterior and wet, mossy yard. The joint is empty. Bruce Phares is working alone. In a way.

The buyer is sleeping on the other side of the planet, in Hong Kong. Phares is about to record a walk-through on his phone to review at her convenience. That's not what he would call it, since real estate agents use the term "walk-through" for the final tour through the house by the buyer's and seller's agents before the property sale closes. This is more like a showing, a look-see, a chance to pique the interest of a buyer who will watch the video hours from now. The listing appeared on the MLS that morning; it's so new that Bruce has only the bare bones facts of the online listing. He is operating from his own visual take on the place.

He looks the living room up and down, fumbles with his phone, then holds it up in landscape aspect, and taps record. He's earned the right to an empty space on the video by being the first agent to request a walk-through after the house was listed last night.

Phares tilts the phone in his hand. At this moment it is more a camera than anything else. "I've got all these systems in this thing that beam me, buzz me, remind me to go back online. A lot of beeping. It starts to feel a little frantic and somewhat robotic at the same time. I like my video work to feel unrushed, solitary even."

Phares knows from experience that this client will stop whatever she's doing—sleeping, drinking, working—to watch the entire video the moment it hits her inbox in Hong Kong. "She's like me," he says. "She likes visuals. She needs to see."

He begins in the empty living room. He squints at the walls, painted a dark terra cotta. He speaks evenly, without anxiety, creating a kind of monologue of location, as he takes his inventory. "This is the Monlake place I mentioned. It's very dark in here, Elaine." He speaks directly to his intended audience. "I imagine you can see that from there. This is the three-hundred square foot living room. We're facing the center of the house. Nice leaded windows. These are original oak floors . . ." he tsks, ". . . with an unfortunate high gloss finish." Words come quickly. His eyes move over every surface as he speaks. The mantel is a handsome Arts & Crafts product. He suspects it may not be original to the house. But "I like it, I like it."

He shifts the view, creates glances around the empty living room. It's beautifully updated, freshly painted. Still, it's easy to tell he is a bit under impressed. Before turning into a dining room he says the living room is "flawlessly appointed with . . ." then he stops and leans in for a closer look. He almost sniffs, and turns the camera away. "Well, a marble-like substance."

He works his way through every room, every hall, up and down both staircases, spreading the screen for close-ups, framing with every zoom of the phone. He does not stop moving, swiveling his hips, falling back for broader views.

He notes every kitchen detail, dispassionately cataloguing the entirety of the real property.

In real estate terms, "real property" refers to the house itself, to the structures, the garage, the guest house, and everything attached to that—the cabinets, the chopping block, the counters, the plumbing, the air-conditioning, the built-ins—anything that can't be moved or taken without the use of tools.

He's listing off what he sees: "Digital closet, subzero refrigerator, it looks like, custom cabinets—beautiful—bathroom double-sink model, with what looks like brass sinks, shower: overhead sun shower, very cool."

Thoroughness and attention are an essential character trait of a good Realtor. Phares is duty bound to pull back the curtain on every property that comes on the market at, or near, the customer's price point. And this one doesn't quite work. But he covers all three floors and the basement in thirteen minutes. Fully narrated. It's a part of the pattern Phares generates for his client; the detail is a means of sharpening his eye for her benefit.

She will give him feedback this evening, after reviewing the tour. She'll have questions. Comments. Phares appreciates them; they'll make the next tour better.

"You build up a rapport with a buyer by finding out what

they want to see, what they respond to," he says. "I'm gaining a shorthand through the virtual walk-through. But I have to cover the whole place, because I don't want to come back out here to look at the shower setup in the master bathroom if she has that question. I'm in the information business. That would be my oversight. These videos are like my memory."

Soon, he's standing in the living room again, about to leave. "By now I know what speaks to her. For instance, she likes light in her living spaces. It's a tall order in a rainy city. And this color scheme is wrong for that. This place is classic, sort of 80s Seattle-dark. Earth tones and lamplight." His gaze is low; he's in evaluation mode. "That was the rage once. Now, it just looks dated."

Outside, late morning thunder rolls. Distant portent. He pockets his phone, hits the lights, and sighs. "I knew the moment I walked in that this place was all wrong for her." In the car, he looks back. "Nice house though," he says. "They'll get a lot more than the asking price."

Will it go for more than a million, a figure that would put it $120,000 over the asking price?

He looks back at the house, its slate roof slick with rain. "I expect so," he says. "That house is certainly right for somebody."

But a million dollars? It feels like a hazy proposition, made in the mind-set of a dream, as if the house bore no real price at all. What's the *purpose* of the asking price in this kind of market?

He holds up a single finger. "Not every house in Seattle goes above the asking price," he says. "The houses in my market sector are in such high demand that the price point is really fluid. Jumpy you might say. The prices change rapidly. Almost from day to day, so these offers are a true test of what the market will bear, which is a lot of pressure on the buyer's agent. That's why the buyer's agent works. Because any offer you make has to be imaginative, aggressive, and well thought out."

So when homes reach the market, Phares does his race to get a look inside, as he has with the Tudor house with the marble-like substance in the living room. When he thinks it will work, he lines up visits by his prospective buyer. Many times, the house will have an obvious disqualifier for the buyer—the bedrooms might be too small or too far apart; the kitchen might be outdated, the backyard might not suit. Elaine, the audience for his design monologue, will find that this one is too dark. They will leave it behind and move to the next showing.

When it works, Phares and the client meet to review

their concerns and enthusiasms. Elaine is prepared to fly in from Hong Kong on short notice. A meeting like that might be on the front lawn of the house in question. It might be online that evening. But it will never be more than a day later. Not in Seattle. Not with Bruce Phares.

6

WAYS TO EARN

"I like to have multiple income streams," Antje Gehrken says. We're in Chicago, tripping past one neighborhood, and down through another. Chicago feels becalmed from this distance. All of it reads as shades of real estate from here. Soon Gehrken slides the car into the express lane, untaxed by the late morning traffic. She's talking about ways she earns money.

"In my twenties, my husband and I owned some rental properties. We did the work ourselves to start. I was used to property management. That was an important, reliable stream of money for us. I learned a lot of lessons there. We ran a family, we had several businesses going besides the band, so none of this real estate stuff was entirely foreign to me."

Although regulations vary from state-to-state, there are only five ways by which real estate agents are expressly allowed to earn compensation from real estate.

- selling real estate (active agency)
- negotiating the sale of real estate (consulting)
- dealing in options on real estate
- procuring leads intended to result in the sale of real estate
- supervising the collection of rent for the use of real estate (property management)

With property management in the mix, Gehrken works at least three of those items at a time—the first, second, and fifth.

"Things go hot and cold in this business, so I broaden my revenue sources for comfort," she says.

It's not uncommon for real estate agents to establish multiple income streams. Bruce Phares owns a property staging business in which he fills empty houses with leased furniture to give prospective buyers a better sense of the human dimensions of a space. Steve Custis owns a property management company with twenty stand-alone rentals.

Gehrken believes that she has another set of skills, developed alongside her husband when they bought and renovated their first home. The Do-It-Yourself gene.

"We didn't have the money to hire a contractor. So I

built out the kitchen myself, replaced the windows myself. I learned how to miter edges and cut compound angles," she says. I watched videos and I did it."

While she's not claiming to be a cabinet-maker, she will assert that having installed cabinets in a kitchen she owned provided her with perspective on the work associated with real property.

"Being a homeowner has been essential for me. The work added up. Now, as an agent, when I walk into a space that needs work, because I've done that work myself, I have that set of insights. I've been a landlord and I've also developed condos, so I have those insights. The best real estate agents bring a broad life perspective, and maybe my experience is a mile wide, inch deep, or whatever that's called," she says, "but it's helped me and it's what I want from the people I hire."

As managing partner of A.R.E. Partners, she does not pay herself in a commission structure, so she isn't a slave to the ups and downs of the housing market. She pays herself, at the advice of an accountant, on a draw from the firm's operating capital. She does assign her agents a standard commission split with the firm and provides them with office and desk space, advertising, and a small support staff.

"There have been times when I haven't had things. My family was made up of immigrants; my mother worked in a factory at night. So, I know what that's like to have very little," she relates. "I'll say it: I like money. I do. I like having things, and I've had no qualms about saying that."

7

THE OFFER

After driving the countryside, perusing neighborhoods in a city, after collecting information on schools or local water, commute times or the condition of the sewers for a client, there comes a point in the life cycle of a real estate agent when the buyer is ready to make an offer. The time between first showing and offer sheet might be months, but in some cases it may be hours. In either case, the role of the real estate agent changes in that moment. After the offer, the work becomes an active contractual negotiation between two agents. "That's when you have to get out of the customer's way in terms of their excitement," Custis says. "But you have to take over too, and stand in the line of fire for them on everything that's about to happen."

When a client is ready to buy, Phares and his partner begin the process of putting together a purchase offer. They will work to determine a proper payment of earnest money (this is a cash payment, made through the buyer's agent, as an advance on the payment at closing. Typically this cash is sacrificed to the seller if the buyer backs out of the contract, or otherwise breaks it). The purchase sheet is a fairly standard form, which includes mandatory components and proposals (including timetables and deadlines) to deal with the buyer's concerns. Otherwise purchase offers generally include:

- The sale price
- The address and sometimes a legal description of the property
- Financing details
- A target date for closing (the actual sale)
- The amount of earnest money accompanying the offer
- Method by which real estate taxes, rents, fuel, water bills, and utilities are to be adjusted (prorated) between buyer and seller at closing
- Provisions about who will pay for title insurance, survey, termite inspections, and the like
- Type of deed that will be granted
- Requirements specific to the state of residence, such as disclosure of specific environmental hazards

- A time limit after which the offer will expire
- Contingencies, such as a window of time in which the buyer might be allowed to secure financing, or secure a satisfactory home inspection

When a purchase offer leaves the real estate agent's office, it is a proposal meant to serve as a blueprint for the final sale. However, it becomes a binding contract upon acceptance by the seller. The challenge for Phares, when representing a buyer, is to craft an offer that protects the needs and concerns of his client while genuinely offering incentives and appeal to the seller by making the process as hassle-free as possible.

So landing a house is not just a matter of being the highest bidder. That would be easy enough. Seattle buyers are generally prequalified with lending institutions weeks before the actual house hunting begins (agents help with banking contacts), or they are paying with cash. So, in this market, buyers further woo sellers with "love letters" about the property, including homemade scrapbooks and mix tapes featuring promises to care for a house, in competing bids for the hearts and minds of sellers.

In most of the country, a "love letter" from a buyer to a seller would seem inconceivable. In the upside-down world of Seattle urban real estate, sellers (who might be parting with the home in which their children were raised, or a family home built by a grandparent) sometimes must be charmed into accepting a buyer's sensibility, their aesthetic, their values. It's an odd and compelling illusion that a house—even a three-bedroom ranch with a converted garage and a cracked pool deck—has an emotional essence served best by promises of a future owner, like the presence of children, the prospect of wine cellars, the certainty of really excellent music piped through the skeleton of its walls. But Phares does not blink regarding love letters. "They are a necessity when a seller is looking at six fairly equal offers for a house that she truly considers a part of her life, a love letter can provide an essential boost to a client's offer," he says. "I'll help my clients write them because they often do the trick."

For Phares, one of the trickiest aspects in the Seattle housing market is scheduling the inspections requested in an accepted purchase offer. Phares has a phalanx of home inspectors, foundation specialists, electricians, construction contractors, and the like who are able to work quickly and reliably to produce written reports that need to be reviewed by his clients in a timely manner. If concerns are raised, these inspections may be used to create points of negotiation with the seller.

What constitutes a full set of inspections? A comprehensive home inspection by a certified expert covers a lot of bases. That's where most real estate agents start. But different regions have different inspections and traditions. Typically these are buyer's costs (home inspections run between $300 and $600). In Seattle, where the financial stakes are so great and time is so tight, home inspections are often done before the offer is made by the buyer. This sort of early inspection reduces the opportunities for delay on closing, thus reducing the anxiety of a seller. So Phares works fast, using one firm he trusts and maintaining good relationships with half a dozen more because scheduling general inspections can be so difficult.

The general inspector usually recommends specific system inspections and the specialists to inspect those in his initial report. Phares or his partner shepherd these inspections through in the period after an offer is accepted, also called the due diligence period. This is an essential time in the life of a home purchase, as the outcome of these inspections may represent a reason to hold up the sale or back out on the contract.

There are as many sorts of inspections as there are potential problems for a listing. Phares can rattle off the inspections he has to consider without much of a pause:

- Pest
- Chimney
- Electrical
- Heating and air-conditioning
- Water systems and plumbing
- Lead paint
- Easements and encroachment
- Roof
- Seismic
- Pool and Spa
- Radon
- Methane
- Asbestos
- Formaldehyde
- Mold

How many inspections should an agent recommend to a buyer? One might as well ask: How long is a piece of string? The answer is theoretical. The benefits are obvious. More information makes a better-informed offer. But buyers sometimes balk at the costs of specific inspections. Many other inspections are required by law—local or federal—or as a requirement of the financing process.

Most significantly for Phares, in a seller's market like

Seattle, the demand for too many inspections after the offer has been accepted can be a disincentive to a seller who's choosing between purchase offers. So Phares tries to identify the problems early, often while helping the buyer settle on an offer price.

"Every house shows different needs," Phares says. "A good agent knows early on what might trip up the value."

A roof truss might need to be upgraded, and the buyer might request that the seller complete this work and absorb the cost before sale. Phares must then become a negotiator, carrying the proposal back to the seller's agent. The seller might offer a financial allowance to cover the cost of the repair. Or, in a market like Seattle's, they might simply refuse. Phares would then go back to his client and strategize a response, such as seeking a financial break elsewhere based on the inspection.

In the case of a seller's market, the speed of processes like these accelerated closings benefit the seller, since they can always refuse and are presumed to have another buyer ready at any time. So one might assume that Phares would assert to his client that the sale was an "as-is" proposition, thereby making inspections less important. Bruce Phares, like many real estate agents, is a creature of conscience. "They have to know what they are getting into," he says. "These are financial choices involving tens of thousands of dollars in upgrades and repairs that the buyer may have to undertake in the months after closing. It can break a young family. I can't live with that."

What the buyer gets in return is the guarantee that the property in question is a house they fully understand, and a sense of confidence that the due diligence performed by their real estate agent will protect them from disaster.

"A house is a big thing in people's lives. The biggest. I don't want them making this giant life decision relying on incomplete information."

8

DUE DILIGENCE

An afternoon spent watching a real estate agent do their paperwork is not like watching someone blow glass. There's not much wonder in the administration of: Transactions. Offer sheet inspections. Disputes. Counter-offers. Contract review. It might seem like the Dickensian purview of a paper-pusher. And sure, in Custis's office, on this one afternoon, there is a large measure of silent, soul-less twenty-first-century email clicking, and a predictable glancing at the monthly sales reports from the national RE/MAX offices. It's a necessary, albeit dull, part of the job, and precision during this stage is critical.

Steve Custis moves slowly through his tasks, smiles, rubs his jaw like the kindest of old men (although he's not yet forty), and speaks with a thread of wonder. In his office chair, straightening up his candy bowl, he's like the happy mayor, finding delight in little bits of news. Nothing seems a particular bother. He'll settle things.

Custis always makes a list. There are eight items today.

"It's just what I'm going to do while I'm sitting here. Now. A list can get longer, sure. Calls pile up. This one has eight items. Maybe there will be ten items when it's all said and done."

Custis never skips an item on his list. "This business has some routine. Lots of compliance. Things you just have to do. I live by the list, whether I want to or not. If anything, I do the things I don't want to do first, because it makes the rest of the list look easier."

The time a real estate agent spends in the office is usually in pursuit of a set of fixed duties surrounding moving a property toward a listing, an offer, or a closing.

In advance of the listing, they include:

- Determination of the home's value in the current market to create a listing price
- Advising the homeowner in readying the home for listing and showings
- Entering the home into the MLS database

Moving toward an offer:

- Market the home to other agents and brokerage members of the MLS
- Market the home in print and other traditional media, as well as on the internet
- Supervise and/or schedule showings of the home
- Report any interest and some feedback from buyers who see the home to the seller

Once the offer is made:

- When a buyer makes an offer, help the seller in negotiations to try and get the price they want and a signed purchase agreement
- Coordinate the process from contract through the closing, including inspections, documents, and other items necessary to close

Today, he'll have some measure of each. Ahead of Custis: Eight phone calls regarding six offer sheets and one potential listing. Custis knows he could reach paydirt in at least three of these transactions in his negotiations today, but he resists the urge to deal with them first.

In advance of each call, he spends time gliding over material he's plainly familiar with, all of it the sum total of three home sales and three purchases, each offer in a different stage. There's nothing unrelated to the work of the day on Custis's desk. No toys or puzzles. Not even many photos. Just a legal pad and pen. The files sit in the center of it all.

"These files just give me a visual idea of what I have to get through today," he says. He crosses items off by acting, not by reshuffling papers or by convincing himself that a stack of work means he's more stressed than anyone else. He emanates a kind of calm, even as his phone starts to ring.

Are people coming in for meetings? It seems a reasonable presumption that a broker might use the time in the office for a face-to-face meeting with clients.

He hovers his hand over the folders, as if he were doing some new-age energy work.

"No one likes face-to-face meetings, except when they're getting checks," he says. "The phone makes everything easier for my clients in this way. I bring the work to them."

The job can lock you down sometimes, he says. "But it's not boring. Every day there's some phone call, some inter-action that's completely unique, where I say, I've never made this particular kind of call before. That's what I like about the real estate business, the sense that you have *never* seen it all."

He points upward, and for a moment I'm afraid he's

going to give thanks to God like an earnest NFL wide receiver after a big win. But then he spins the finger in an upward circle, indicating the craziness of the everyday. "All this began earlier in the week," he says, "and now some of it comes to an end."

In a real estate deal, once the purchase agreement is set, it becomes a binding contract. Both the buyer's agent and the seller's agent then work to keep the agreement in place, by laying out clear contingencies and guarding the contracts to keep them from going into default. These are the calls that occupy Custis today. He and the other agents guard against cancellation of the contract, which can only occur in one of the following circumstances:

- The buyer fails to pay earnest money on time
- The buyer or seller fails to return signed disclosure forms on time
- The buyer or seller cancels the sale after all contingencies have been removed
- The seller does not complete contractually obligated work on the property
- The seller prevents access for inspection or final walk-through
- The seller does not move out on time

The respective agents, buyer and seller, enter this negotiation by shifting to the role of counselor and secretary
during the period of due diligence after signing and before
closing. Phone calls touching base and reminders via text are
the best hedge against missed deadlines with clients. Often
buyers will be too anxious to take possession of a property
and sellers may drag their feet on repairs or upgrades they
agreed to do in the heat of the sale. Both agents benefit by
keeping things on track and completed by the agreed upon
date. Small moments of negotiation and clarification are
common at this time. Never is there direct contact between
the buyer and seller. All communication is done agent-to-
agent. The client is then consulted.

Today Custis has to take on his own client, who went
onto the property of the house he is buying for an inspection, and used the access granted for the inspection to dig
holes around the septic system to locate a clean-out valve.
The seller's agent reported to Custis this morning that
three large holes were left unfilled, and the appraiser was
scheduled to come back within forty-eight hours. The seller's agent was understanding, but was counting on Custis to
convince his client that his behavior regarding the inspection of the plumbing and septic system was explicitly outside the bounds of the contract, since access to that system

was not granted, and that it should be remediated. Custis knows that his client is a strong personality, and that he won't respond to legalistic language.

"This one falls in the realm of dumb," he says. "I just have to keep everything cool." Custis looks at the caller ID and gives me a little upnod. "I just try to handle these situations using some love."

The buyer answers, knowing full well it's Custis on the other end. Such is the intimacy of caller ID. "How's it going, Steve?"

"What's up, Dan?" Custis rubs his chin and looks down at the phone. "Well, hopefully you still have a shovel handy."

It's not an accusation. Not a trap. It's just enough to get a laugh and launch straight into the middle of things. Custis knows his context. And the buyer doesn't feign ignorance. He jumps right in.

"Oh, screw them!" he says.

At that, Custis laughs outright. "Oh yeah. They weren't real happy about it," Custis says. "They just want the holes filled back in."

The client goes quiet then. In about the quickest retreat ever, he surprisingly peeps: "Okay." Maybe this won't be so hard after all.

Custis nods. "And I don't know if you have time, but they

said there was mud in the house and they didn't know if that was you." He pauses. "I told them it could've been the inspector."

"Well, we were all tracking mud in the house. Them too."

"Yeah, I told them that," Custis affirms. "But, if you can, definitely . . . just maybe . . . fill in those swimming pools that you dug."

They share a laugh, but then the client sighs. "Steve, I'm ten days from buying the place. I don't understand why they care. I mean, do they really think the sale isn't gonna go to close?"

A diverse set of negotiating skills is an essential strength of good agents. Arguments like this tend to exacerbate people's pride or fear. They're not always easy. A buyer is rarely completely sure that he or she is doing the right thing in making this large purchase; at this very moment, they may be looking for an out, whereas a seller generally feels that it will be difficult to get through the due diligence without being made to pay for repairs and upgrades he wants nothing to do with. The real estate agent has to be one part crisis counselor and one part police officer, always casting an ear for what triggers outsized responses from either party. The challenge for Custis is to communicate in a manner that doesn't threaten the ego of his client, while producing the desired result: get the holes filled in.

But the client continues with the pushback. "Steve, is this not something we could argue a little bit? 'Cause, I mean, I'm . . ."

Custis faces the phone, pinching one eye against the progress of this thing. He smiles broadly, to indicate that he is positively lighthearted about things.

"This is a huge part of . . ." the client continues, then suddenly states: "I just don't think I'm gonna be able to let this go, really."

Custis pauses, but does not allow silence to take over. He knows better than to give that kind of dramatic power to a reticent client. "Here's their concern and it's a valid concern. The appraiser's going back out there Wednesday. If, for some reason, he sees those holes, and he flags the septic for being in disrepair, that fact will be in the appraisal, and then if our deal doesn't close, they are stuck with an appraisal that mentions that the septic system could have issues because someone's been digging it up." The client is silent this time. "I definitely understand their concern," Custis says, "since it could be something that goes forward to the next customer."

The client growls a little, but Custis seems to take no notice.

"I did tell them that you were a solid buyer, that it was a solid deal," Custis reassures him.

The client stammers, "All I'm saying . . . all I'm saying, and I'm not trying to make an argument, Steve, like, I don't want to piss people off. But I want them to understand that, you know, we're very solid buyers and I already know that I am going to have to dig at least one of those holes back up again."

Custis shrugs. "Yeah. Gotcha. Well here's what we'll do: go fill in the two today and I'll leave a note for the sellers and the appraiser saying, 'Hey, disregard the hole in the yard. We were trying to find the clean out for the septic tank."

The buyer *tsks* then. "Man, you could argue a bear out from facedown in a honey pot," he says. "I mean, that's fine. I'll do it."

"I'll tell you what," Custis says, bearing down on his point. "If it comes to that point, I will personally fill in the third hole for you so that you don't have to come back out there."

The buyer gives a little hiccup at that. "The hell you will," he says. Then they both laugh.

"But I don't think that it will come to that," Custis says. "This sale is going through." Then Custis says his goodbyes, speaking in the positive, affirming the plan, reasserting the friendship, the partnership.

How does it not drive him crazy? Is that just the cost of doing business with your friends?

"I'd never met him before this listing," he says.

He crosses out on item on his list, then shoots an email to the seller's agent.

"I've found that when property changes hands, there are always these moments when one party or the other wants to claim things," he says. "Real estate is kind of territorial."

CUSTIS'S NEXT CALL IS a deal gone bad.

His seller had a six hundred thousand dollar house in the neighboring county. A buyer came forward, they took the offer. "Then two days went by, then four days went by, then six days, and the buyer never submitted his earnest money." Earnest money is cash presented by the buyer at the offering to assure good faith. It's typically collected with the purchase offer by the seller's agent, then put in escrow and applied to the sale price at closing. That may be sacrificed if the deal goes sour before closing. The offer is not valid until the earnest money is agreed upon, provided, and accepted.

But this buyer asked for extra time and then didn't provide it. "It was supposed to be a cash deal too, with six thousand dollars in earnest money," Custis says. One percent of the purchase price is a very low amount of earnest money to agree to, but cash offers are rare enough that sellers sometimes accept less than the conventional 5 percent or 10 percent ask. Custis informed the buyer that the deal was not in effect until they had their hands on the earnest money, and began calling the buyer's agent to request the cash.

This was when the mistake was made. "So, then my seller moves out of the house prematurely," Custis says. "I wish he would have waited, but he was concerned about the weather, all that snow about a month ago. And then there was no earnest money, and [there were] no completed inspections. Nothing. He moved too fast. It just wasn't time to move out."

Then the deal fell through, because the buyer never did submit his earnest money. "He got into some legal trouble," Custis says. He shrugs. "There's a warrant out for his arrest."

So the seller should have never moved out, that much is clear. I ask: "Was it a mistake on your part, leaving without a check?"

Custis purses his lips. Collection of earnest money *is* the responsibility of the buyer's agent. In this case, that agent did not bring the check, or cash, to Custis. "The mistake I made was probably not explicitly saying to my seller, *Wait, don't do anything, we don't have a deal yet, really.* And before the weekend came, he moved. When I see him he says, 'Hey, I know I moved out before you said to.'" Custis shrugs. He wishes it hadn't happened. "Maybe I didn't warn him strongly enough," he says. "You could consider that a mistake."

What about this phone call telling your client the deal is over? Do you dread this one? Is he going to yell at you?

Custis gives this a little chinwag. "No, it's okay even if he does. We're cool. Like I said, everything with love in your heart. I truly, I try to treat people like my friends."

When he makes the call the seller answers, shouting, "Steve Custis!"

Custis replies, shouting too. "What are you doing?"

Without pause, the seller says, "Sitting here, not doing a damned thing for forty-five minutes."

"I've got some updates for you," Custis says, "Did you get my email this morning?"

"I did," the speaker says. The email had intimated that the deal had likely fallen through.

"That is literally all I have at this point." He delivers the bad news. "So, that's over." Silence. Then he asks, "How do you feel?"

Without missing a beat, the seller then says, "I want to keep moving forward by letting them know I just got another . . ."

"Another offer?"

"Yup!" the seller says, loud enough, happy enough that his voice squeaks. He's heard from the second buyer this morning, And just like that, the terms shift and the day is flipped. Good times overtake bad times. Now the busted deal can just wither away. Or better still, Custis realizes, it can be used as a tactic to motivate this new buyer. Such is the roller coaster of real estate.

Custis laughs. He vets the terms of the new offer, asks about another showing. Double-checks. Then pauses. He's satisfied for now. The new buyer will present an offer this evening. "Okay, all right. Well then, I'm gonna call each Realtor and let them both know about the existence of the other one." Custis keeps on, "And I'm gonna tell 'em we're ready to dance, so the first one that starts playing music, we'll start stepping."

With that, he hangs up. "Every day," he says, without looking at me, "something new."

He calls both of the other Realtors. The first one he doesn't know. "Some fella two counties over," he says. "He's new." He leaves a message. This is a big swing. Custis went from a lost offer, no earnest money, and no commission, to a cash offer 5 percent above sale price in a matter of a phone call.

Steve is the principal in his firm. As the listing agent for the seller, he'll take down a full 3 percent commission for a cash sale of $630,000. $18,900. Nice swing. Buyer's market indeed. Then he calls the second Realtor, a woman from a town called Clayton, and lets her know how quickly things changed.

Real estate agents are not lawyers; they do not practice contract law. But a binding sale contract is serious business, and conscientious real estate agents like Phares feel the pressure that comes with fine-tuning the details. Phares has a partner in his office who reviews offers before they go out. And his wife (a former real estate agent herself) will double-check him. Phares is fairly well defined by his anxiety about not letting down his client. "Buying and selling in this market represents a great deal of money," he says. "I have people buying their first houses, which may end up being their only houses. I consider it a moral obligation, and professional obligation, to get things right."

But mistakes are inevitable. What happens then? How has Phares dealt with that?

Phares thinks awhile.

"Say you write a contract on behalf of a buyer, and you have a five-day time period to work in," Phares says, "And during that time period, you have to do a certain number of items of due diligence. Inspections, certificates, clearances. Me, I mean. It's my job then to bring in people who can deal the information to your buyer so they can make the decision. And the mistake then would be that I did not make the appointments in time to get those people there. Maybe I called too late, or failed to return some breezy text. And then I come up against the deadline and my buyers don't have the information that should have been there for them, or even, just stuff that's standard practice. And now I simply was negligent in remembering to make a call, because I may have procrastinated about making the phone calls." His eyes widen. He looks duly concerned. "Or maybe I was too nervous to call a contractor I didn't know for the first time. Making this the worst sort of mistake. They lose the house they want. The earnest money. The time." He tilts his head, considers the street and a broad storefront window. "Or worse," he says, "they end up buying a house that isn't right somehow."

Phares shudders, and pulls through the light. "Yeah, so that would be a mistake."

He's looking for a parking space, a little mournfully. His

thoughts trouble him. He drives straight past two open slots. "And then, the question is what would I do?" He hits the brakes hard, and backs up for a spot, pulls in. He speaks only after he's put the car in park. "I would freak out," he says. "I would be overcome by massive self-loathing and I would get ahold of my clients. I'm sure I'd want to cry. Tell them I'm really sorry, I really fucked up. I just dropped the ball on this and we're in a horrible situation. And I'd tell them myself."

He gets out of the car then, buttons his coat against the wind, and carries on. Moments later, he admits that he likes being answerable for himself and his performance. He doesn't have a boss, an employer, or someone to cover for him. This is how he wants it. "That's what's great about this business. You always have to face the truth. Mistakes do happen. You can survive," he says. "But liars don't last long in real estate."

9

THE CLOSING

In twelfth-century Europe, real estate transfers were often witnessed, and not recorded in written fashion. The act signifying the transfer was known as "The Livery of Seisen." Although it sounds a little like the name of a municipal horse stable in central Norway, the Livery of Seisen was a symbolic public event, performed within sight of the land in question, involving a highly public ritual called "the turf and twig ceremony." The gist of that ceremony involved the seller, or "feoffor," declaring that the land was his to give and handing the buyer or "foeffee" a bag of dirt, or a twig, or a ring.

This act, this "deed," was the primary record of the land transfer. Livery of Seisen translates as "delivery of possession," which you can almost hear if you slur the words. The process is also known as decree by deed, which is why we call the primary legal record of ownership a "deed." In any case, there were always lots of witnesses to this ceremony. Presumably none of them ever forgot the time one guy gave the other guy a bag of dirt, because written records were not kept.

Today? Not so much. The "closing" represents the conclusion of the real estate sales process and written records are the muscle of today's real estate closings. In the weeks prior, these meetings act as a deadline for each party in the contract to come in to compliance with the requirements of the document. Financing must be acquired, repairs made, inspections passed. The two agents will communicate throughout this time, working together, and a meeting will generally take place in a conference room in the offices of a title company. It involves a gathering of the principle parties—the buyer, the seller, their representative real estate agents, and a title officer. The title officer, or their representative, guides the buyer, then the seller through the signing of numerous documents, sometimes in duplicate or triplicate.

"Closings are easy," Steve Custis told me. "You're studying your own performance every moment up until then. And you're double-checking the other agent. It's the one time you act like a team." Everybody needs to understand each document, he says. The clients need to be familiar with every step about what's about to happen. So the room moves at the pace set by the title officer, who has spent the last few weeks checking the title to be sure it is unencumbered by liens or levees, and has contacted the banks in question to confirm the financing, as well as the officers of the municipality to be sure the taxes are paid, or will be paid at closing. "Everybody wants it done," he says.

Antje Gehrken finds closings soothing. The conference rooms feel like libraries. "They have a kind of silence to them that is pretty welcome in this business," she says.

And Bruce Phares? "Closings can be worrisome," he says. "For me anyway. I mean: it's the last possible moment for someone—anyone—to lose their mind and throw a wrench into the works. Or just change their mind, right there in the last moments. But I know that if I've done my job, everyone is walking out with a check. And my guys, my clients, they're holding the keys to their next chapter, or to the rest of their lives, and that is highly, highly satisfying." He sighs. "At some point, you gotta love a check with your name on it."

10

TO-DO: FIND A MENTOR

Antje Gehrken didn't have a boss when she was in her band. It was simply her band. She never had someone else passing down assignments, or leading her through some kind of apprenticeship. She sat down and figured the problems herself, then took the lead with the other band members, made rules, established expectations. Some of it worked. It was a kind of management, created by the need for self-discipline. Growth. Profit, even. That sort of leadership carries over well into a work environment like a real estate office, which demands self-motivated problem solvers. When she started her brokerage, she didn't have a supervisor saying *here's how you do this*, or *here's what I want you to do*. She had to figure it out on her own again.

That's the real estate way.

Individual real estate agents often work in a solitary fashion. Essentially, they are independent contractors, set up and supported by the agency to generate business for themselves. Months can pass before the money starts to show up from closings. Every other agent in the office is a competitor for your business. When the market sags, the career can become financially fraught. In larger firms and national franchise offices, office fees can accumulate and eat into the already rare commission checks. Leads get used up. Advertising on a fixed budget only goes so far in generating contacts. For a new agent, after the first few weeks of relative calm, the quiet of a phone that doesn't ring only makes the endeavor feel more risky and dispiriting.

Gehrken insists that only an agent can save another agent.

"But I'll tell you what, when I started my brokerage, I consciously picked a mentor of my own, someone very special, whom I could talk to and see what the best way to do this or that was. She was a broker too, at a competing agency. And I ate up her time. I called her at work, and at home. I ran stuff by her. You can't work in this business without a senior person you trust. Especially when you're working for yourself." One of the first jobs for any new agent, she says, is to find someone to trust.

She tries to make herself available too. "And now, when I hire brokers to work for me, one of the things I try to do is mentor them, touch base with them, inspire and motivate," she says, holding up a finger because she missed a freeway exit. She acknowledges the deep self-interest involved in the relationship. She runs the agency; she splits commissions with her agents. "Providing good guidance is easy, because frankly I'm doing it for myself."

How does the inspiration stuff work?

"I note their habits. I try to keep track of where they are in the sales process. I don't contain my enthusiasm when they succeed, and I prod them gently when they fail. Or fail to act." She smiles. Anyone can get caught up in self-doubt, or fail to follow up on a lead because it's simply too enervating to make yet another call to someone who doesn't know you, doesn't even want to. "It's like being an older sibling," she says. "Gentle or firm, there are still times when I just look at them and say: 'Do *something. Do* it.'"

"You have to call people, Tom," Bruce Phares says, without looking up, when I ask him what his list would say. "You have to ask for help."

"When a person starts, there have to be people who can be counted on. So you'd better pick a reliable mentor, because you're going to be running in there to double-check everything." This person might be the broker who hired you. But it might be an agent in the office you trust to be another set of eyes. Phares believes you have to have someone to lean on. "You aren't going to pull off your first closings without someone looking over your processes."

"You *absolutely* need a mentor," Bruce Phares says, asserting that's why people come into *existing* real estate firms. The support they get from other working agents is what gives them the true license to set out on their own. "This is a learn-on-your-feet, fly-by-the-seat-of-your-pants kind of job. You'll need help."

"And get a good partner," he says. "I have one. And that's why my wife's name is still on our business. My wife was driven out by the use of cell phones and online forms. She likes to see things finished, crossed off the list. I have this mind . . ." He taps his index finger into his temple then, hard enough that it might have hurt. "I'm an ADHD brain. I jump around, I like moving. I enjoy things frantic. And that's why the phone works for me, because I gravitate toward games and puzzles. My wife absolutely hates that stuff. My partner is also a to-do list person."

"Before the phone was like this," he says, holding his cell phone up like a lab specimen, intensely small and capable. "I used to kind of hand-draw my calendars, because I realized that if I wanted to have excitement about my calendar, I had to have some colors."

He laughs thinking about it. "You could pretty much tell

how I was feeling about myself by how my calendar looked on a monthly basis. I would work on all these lists and get them going, and then I would get about halfway through. I would pick it up and it wouldn't mean anything, which is not good."

"My wife, my business partner, and my partner in musical performance—they saved me," he says, shaking his head. He crumples up a sandwich bag and we stand. He's got more work ahead. "In my real estate work, there's always someone partnered up with you, or against you, asking you questions or negotiating. Find a partner who fills in your gaps, and pay attention to your habits." He remembers something then, and sets the alarm on his phone. He mumbles to himself then. "You work for yourself in this business," he says, "But the thing is, a real estate agent is never really alone when he's working."

START NOW

Okay, now.

"The thing I would tell someone who is getting into the field?" Antje Gehrken says. We're sitting in the empty apartment, the one she's listing for sale tomorrow, just above Belmont. The radiators kick on, and she bears down on her point.

"Start now. Now. Before you even take a class. It's all about the networking and who you know. Look around you. Gauge your competition. Everybody knows a real estate agent. Everybody's got a sister, or a friend from martial arts class, who's a real estate agent. So those are the people you're going to be up against. The same people I'm up against. You might as well get to know them now. Start now. Make contacts. Create leads. Go on showings. Act like an agent. Do it. Right now."

She grabs her jacket from a counter in the kitchen, and we make ready to leave. Out into the city, toward her Mercedes.

The best lesson she learned? She realizes it as we stand waiting for the elevator. It's this: "Don't work for the commission," she says. "Work for the sale."

How's that?

"Look, two years ago I closed a house for $129,000. It was a lot of work for very, very little money (less than a $4,000 commission split). But it was this first-time homebuyer and he never anticipated how hard it might be. And it was my listing, and he didn't have any representation. I introduced him to the lender and found a program for him to finance through. So I helped him, gratis." She waves her hand, at the praise that might follow. No, no. "Agents do this all the time," she says. "It's not all cutthroat stuff up in this business."

"And now, years later, guess what? I'm helping him find

his next one. I'll help him buy it, and someday I'll help him sell it." When the doors close behind us, she stretches her back and speaks into the empty grip of the elevator. "That first commission meant nothing. The sale is what matters," she says. "The sale is what lasts. *Work for the sale.*"

On the street, we stand together as she loads her stuff in the trunk and offers a handshake. She glances at the sky, shades her eyes, then looks into the trunk. It looks now like it might snow. Chicago. "This isn't my only car. I actually have an old beater too," she explains. "Most of the time, I just go with that." She raps on the back window of the Mercedes with one knuckle. "Customers hate it when I drive up in this thing. Expensive cars bring up a lot of judgments. When you're a real estate agent, people should be able to see who you really are."

She offers a little cringe then, tilting her head. "So, depending on who you're working with," she says, "maybe don't drive a Mercedes."

FORM GOOD HABITS

AT MOORE'S BAR, CUSTIS listens to a list of his best habits, which I culled from the way he plowed through those phone calls, from the other lunches we've shared, from our drives through the county. He makes me stop before I read the first item and thinks for a while. The exercise seems immodest to him. "There was plenty of failure," he says. "I came into this with a lot of really dumb habits. And I've still got bad habits just like everybody else."

"Come on," I tell him. "You're good at what you do. These aren't your only habits." Then we order lunch. Joy recommends the special. Custis concurs. Then he blankly watches golf highlights over my shoulder. Finally, he says, "All right. Let me hear this manifesto."

1. Pick up the phone. Return every call quickly.

He stops me then. "But I've come to believe, for example, that every contact, every call is a kind of opportunity. You know, maybe you get to move on. Just cut bait. Resolve things." Then he apologizes and motions for me to go ahead.

2. Names matter. Learn the names.
3. Keep an uncluttered workspace.
4. Make a list. Keep it simple.
5. But always review your material before making that call.

6. Do nothing else while you're on a call. Keep your hands on your desk.

"I didn't know I did that," he says. "I like that: Flat on your desk."

7. Stay calm! Keep others calm.
8. Don't be afraid to say *I don't know.*
9. Don't stop working until you've crossed out every item on that list.
10. Everything with love in your heart.

All the wide grins, the massive grip of his handshakes, his legitimate acceptance of the eccentricity of others, is wrapped like chain mail around this guy's being. He's a true believer in the work. The negotiator of place. He knows this place and he knows his job, and he wants to know you.

"That's good list," he says. "You really think I do all that?"

"That's probably just the start of it," I said. "That's just what I observed."

"I don't know," he says, "It's not very pragmatic. It all seems pretty complicated."

Pragmatic? Seriously? I really don't know how it could get any simpler.

The job comes down to one thing. "Really, what I love about selling real estate is that the better I treat people in the way I do my own work, the better the work pays," he says.

"So, it's the money?" I say.

He laughs, filling the whole bar with the sound. "Right! Right! I just like the money!"

When we stand, I reach for a handshake and his cell phone rings. He looks at the number. "I have to take this," he says. "I'm sorry." He fist-bumps me, phone clamoring in his hand.

"Pick up the phone," I say, echoing habit 1 on the list. "I appreciate it, Steve," I say.

He gives me an upnod, and sits back down to take the call. "I appreciate you," he says. I believe him.

DOUBLE-CHECK EVERYTHING

ANTJE GEHRKEN PARALLEL PARKS that Mercedes, and now the lakeside wind saws through her as she walks east toward the water. This is Gehrken's newest listing, a

2,200-square foot, two-bedroom apartment on the seventh floor in a wing of the apartment building a block or two above Belmont Avenue. She's there to be sure it's ready for a showing that afternoon, checking the lockbox placement, examining a room she's had painted, making sure a pile of drop cloths has been moved out. It's a major property for her, with nearly a $400,000 asking price, in a neighborhood where she wants more listings. Her rule: double-check everything.

On the elevator ride up, Gehrken notes a particular quirk of the property. The elevator opens to a private lobby for each apartment in the wing. "They each get to decorate the lobby for their own floor," she says. "People put a lot of work into it." She goes to the fourteenth floor and stops at every floor going down to the seventh. The fourteenth floor is elegantly Scandinavian. The thirteenth seems unimproved since the late 50s. On twelve, the motif is black and white, sort of English mod. Eleven is austere Victorian. Ten: stark modernism. Nine: Vampire Hunters. Eight: Cubs. It makes her laugh.

A real estate agent has to love the idiosyncrasies of a property, be an enthusiast of the place. She wouldn't do a showing of the apartment on seven without taking her prospective buyer through the lobby themes. "If that doesn't crack you up, then maybe you don't need to live in the city," she says when we stop on seven.

The apartment is large, with freshly buffed hardwood floors and large windows. It is empty. "This is a choice listing for us," she says. "I love the kitchen, there's a butler's pantry. But I think a buyer will want to pull everything out and start over." She gets a phone call as we're standing there and retreats to an empty bedroom to take it.

When she returns, she seems downcast. Good news or bad news, she won't say. She allows that she's not sorry she took the call. "People treat everyone who uses a cell phone like they're a distracted teenager. My phone is my tool. And a Realtor has to act. Realtors make decisions. She has to help her clients act. I don't mean acting off the cuff, not being thoughtful about decisions, but decisions need to be made. The phone matters."

"I don't always know what a phone call will bring. Maybe the buyer loses interest when the furniture is out of the house, or the state won't drop a tax lien in time for closing. Whatever. And the closing is two days away, and the client really needs possession of the house. They have nowhere to go. And the agent needs the money too. But now everything is kind of, well, screwed." Gehrken is speaking levelly now, her voice echoing into the empty living space.

The Realtor can't be too afraid of disaster, because that's the job. Disaster is her business. "You can't go to work on it, until you pick up the phone," she says. "Always pick up. Always."

"Weirdly, I've been told I come across as being just very confident. Or motivated, driven, whatever it is that some people don't like in women. That gets used against me all the time. But I've learned it's best that I own up to fear. I just say what's on my mind. I just tell the other party precisely what I'm afraid of. Fear is fine. People don't expect candor in moments of doubt." She gathers her files from the hardwood floor. If things go right, she will reintroduce the rhythms of life into this emptiness later this week. Next week at the latest.

KNOW YOUR PLACE

BRUCE PHARES TAKES A moment to sit down by the houseboats in a harbor on Lake Union. His office is nearby, maybe three blocks away. This bench is a place he sneaks out to with a half sandwich. Here's where he comes to take one more look at the lives Seattle people build for themselves, and the places where they choose to live them out.

His gaze bumps along the tilted docks, a washed-out burger joint by the entrance, the rusted barrels tucked in along chain-link fence line and the gleaming, incongruent Audis wheeled in between.

He misses old Seattle. "It was a working man's town. The houses were owned by factory workers, sawmill guys, airline mechanics." The factory behind us has been retooled as headquarters of an operation called Zymogenetics. So it feels a long way from the era of two-cycle engine repair, even though that's the service featured on the nearby dock. Across the water, there's a traffic artery filling up at midday. "But you can just barely see that old city," he says, his voice dropping into a speculative register. Isn't all this—the gentrification, the churning reinvention of commercial spaces, the new roadways unwisely appended to the old ones, parking lots packed in by more parking lots—isn't it all simply the price tag that goes along with a feverish rise of property values? The new city rises up to replace the old. Isn't he a part of all that? Isn't this what drives the feverish pace of his work?

"You have to know place. And a place never really stays the same." Phares sighs. "This kind of growth is both the benefit and the cost of what's happening."

He pauses a moment, and lowers his gaze along the far

shore. "Well, I know how strangely upside-down this market has become, and I don't want to sound ungrateful, or even unaware of what my clients have done for the city, for me." He pauses. "I know things about myself. In my head, I'm still a musician, a guy who believes he's living on the music he makes."

How is that ungrateful? I ask.

"It's just some part of me despises wealth," he says.

He looks utterly concerned at the moment. He's an anxious guy. Solid and trustworthy. Thoughtful. He's got his eyes on the water, the distant shore, the slow chains of traffic. "In a city, money brings damage and repair," he says. "You want to be part of one, and not the other. But at this speed, how can you tell them apart?"

He leans forward, elbows on knees. "I know this place," Bruce Phares says. "This was a small city."

You'd expect to hear a boat bell ring, but this has to be the quietest boatyard in history. You can't hear the water. No motors. The houseboats don't even rock. The only noise, as ever, is the distant growl of the I-5 behind us.

Bruce Phares will tell you, there were glaciers here once.

APPENDIX

CURRENT STATISTICS AND DEMOGRAPHICS

U.S. Bureau of Labor Statistics, *Real Estate Brokers and Sales Agents Occupational Outlook Handbook*, September 2018, https://www.bls.gov/ooh/sales/real-estate-brokers-and -sales-agents.htm.

National Association of Realtors, "Quick Real Estate Statistics," May 2018, https://www.nar.realtor/research-and -statistics/quick-real-estate-statistics.

FREQUENTLY ASKED QUESTIONS
(AND THEIR ANSWERS)

Trulia: www.trulia.com

GENERAL RESOURCES

Real Estate Express: www.realestateexpress.com
National Association of Realtors: www.nar.com
Realtor.com

SALARY, COMPENSATION, COMMISSIONS, AND FEES

"Real Estate Agent Salaries," Indeed.com, https://www.indeed.com/salaries/Real-Estate-Agent-Salaries.

"5 Reasons Agents Love a Real Estate Career," Real Estate Express, https:// www.realestateexpress.com/career-hub/become-a-real-estate-agent/5-reasons-agents-love-a-real-estate-career/.

John Stark, "So You Want to Be a Real Estate Agent," Next Avenue.com, March 20, 2015, https://www.nextavenue.org/so-you-want-be-real-estate-agent/.

Julie Ryan Evans, "Real Estate Agent Fees: Who Pays the Bill?", Realtor.com, June 13, 2017, https://www.realtor.com//advice/finance/realtor-fees-closing-costs/.

LICENSING REQUIREMENTS

Kapre.com: Kapre.com/real-estate-courses

An excellent, comprehensive resource outlining general requirements, examinations, and continuing education requirements on a state-by-state basis (this is a commercial site).

TOOLS FOR WORKING IN REAL ESTATE

The Blogs at Keller Williams.com

Excellent resources for potential clients and agents, following trends in the market, the real estate career, and beyond, including leads, leverage, technology, and marketing/branding (commercial site).

Jason Fox Blog: Jasonfox.me
Terrific resources for the DIY Realtor

The Blogs at Speaking of Real Estate.com: http://speaking ofrealestate.blogs.realtor.org/
Excellent discussions of ethics, marketing, communication, and outreach, given as a teaser in preparation for joining the National Association of Realtors.

ACKNOWLEDGMENTS

In crafting this book, I spoke to twenty-four real estate agents in twelve different states. I found each of them to be principled, forthright, honest, and highly ethical representatives of their profession. Thank you. In particular, of course, I'd like to thank the subjects of this volume—Bruce Phares, Antje Gehrken, and Steve Custis. They generously revealed their lives and processes to me, even when I may have asked too much. Each was a teacher and advisor in their own way. I also appreciate the help I got from Maria Dickman at the Chicago Area Realtors Association. Thanks to Seattle friends Dave and Katie Seawell, David Crouse, and Bonnie Whiting. Further thanks to my terrific editors, Karyn Marcus, Stuart Roberts, and, as always, to my dearest darling: Chris White. Brian Langdoc was a moderate amount of help as well. (I kid!)

ABOUT THE AUTHOR

TOM CHIARELLA lives and works in Bainbridge, Indiana, which he calls the city of the future. He worked for twenty years as writer-at-large for *Esquire* magazine. His work has also appeared in the *New Yorker*, *Golf* magazine, *Popular Mechanics*, *Story*, *Chicago*, *Golf Digest*, *Euroman*, *O: The Oprah Magazine*, *Runner's World*, Medium, and elsewhere. He the author of *Foley's Luck*, *Thursday's Game*, and *Writing Dialogue*. He is professor emeritus of English at DePauw University. He and his wife own that house by the covered bridge.